Ideology and Political Life

D1040612

Ideology and Political Life

Kenneth R. Hoover
University of Wisconsin—Parkside

Brooks/Cole Publishing Company
Monterey, California

Brooks/Cole Publishing Company
A Division of Wadsworth, Inc.
© 1987 by Wadsworth, Inc., Belmont, California 94002. All rights reserved. No part of this book may be reproduced, stored in a retrieval system, or transcribed, in any form or by any means—electronic, mechanical, photocopying, recording or otherwise—without the prior written permission of the publisher, Brooks/Cole Publishing Company, Monterey, California 93940, a division of Wadsworth, Inc.

Printed in the United States of America
10 9 8 7 6 5 4 3 2 1

Library of Congress Cataloging in Publication Data

Hoover, Kenneth R. [date]
   Ideology and political life.

   Bibliography: p.
   Includes index.
   1. Political science—History.   2. Ideology.
I. Title.
JA81.H63   1986   320.5   86-18392
ISBN 0-534-06996-7

Sponsoring Editor: *Cynthia C. Stormer*
Editorial Assistant: *Maria Rosillo Alsadi*
Production Editor: *Penelope Sky*
Manuscript Editor: *Meredy Amyx*
Permissions Editor: *Mary Kay Hancharick*
Interior and Cover Design: *Katherine Minerva*
Cover Illustration: *David Aguero*
Art Coordinator: *Lisa Torri*
Interior Illustration: *Maggie Stevens*
Typesetting: *Kachina Typesetting Inc., Tempe, Arizona*
Printing and Binding: *Malloy Lithographing, Inc., Ann Arbor, Michigan*

To Andrew Lee Hoover
and Erin Elizabeth Hoover

PREFACE

This book presents the key ideologies involved in contemporary American life. For the student of politics, it will serve as a basic text on the meanings of these ideologies. The reader will have the chance to confront each ideology in its own terms, and then to understand its origins, development, and current political significance. In the final chapter, I have summarized some important characteristics of ideologies and commented on how they affect our relationship to politics.

Each chapter begins with a simplified description of the image of political life that can be derived from one ideology. The second part is an analysis designed to unfold the assumptions, shifts of meaning, and experimentation that went into the development of the image. The images of political life are, in a sense, utopias written from the point of view of specific ideologies. Some ideologies can't be reduced to a single image. For example, contrasting images are developed to illustrate two different versions of conservatism: libertarian and traditionalist.

The analytical part of each chapter explores how the ideas emerged, how they are applied to contemporary political issues, and major criticisms. The history of each ideology is organized primarily by introducing new themes rather than by concentrating on dates, names of theorists, or historical epochs, which are brought in only as they become relevant to the development of the ideas. A brief outline at the beginning of each chapter anticipates the structure of the discussion.

■ Acknowledgments

A book of this kind reflects the summation of many influences: twenty years of teaching, reading, and writing about political ideas; innumerable discussions with students; the instruction of others; the critiques of colleagues; and the observation of political life at home and in visits to Great Britain, Canada, Mexico, Europe, and the Soviet Union. Any acknowledgment of names must therefore be incomplete.

I especially want to thank those who read manuscript chapters and provided comments: Terence Ball, University of Minnesota; Barbara Callaway, Rutgers University; Laura Gellott, University of Wisconsin—Parkside; Lawrence Giel, Ferris State College; Jerome Hanus, American University; Ian Harris, University of Wisconsin—Milwaukee; Suzanne Jacobitti, Southern Illinois University; Mark Kann, University of Southern California; Joseph Larkin, University of Wisconsin—Parkside; Marcus Pohlmann and Susan Power, Arkansas State University; and Donald Whistler, University of Central Kansas. They bear a good measure of credit for what is here, and no responsibility for my final choices of content and argument.

The influence of certain teachers lasts through the years; they include Murray Edelman and Robert Booth Fowler, University of Wisconsin—Madison; Thomas Landon Thorson, Indiana University at South Bend; Kenneth Dolbeare, Evergreen State College; Michael Oakeshott, the London School of Economics and Political Science; and Robert Irrmann and Milton Feder, Beloit College.

Craig Barth of Brooks/Cole served as Executive Editor for the project, and as Acting Political Science Editor at the completion of the manuscript. Marquita Fleming took the initiative as Political Science Editor, and Marie Kent, Cindy Stormer, and Amy Mayfield helped along the way. My thanks to them, and to Production Editor Penelope Sky and her fine colleagues at Brooks/Cole.

The University of Wisconsin—Parkside supported the writing of this book in many ways, most particularly by awarding a sabbatical leave for the fall of 1985. For assistance in manuscript preparation, and some interesting comments in the process, I am very grateful to Kari Dixon, Kim Plache, and Essie Zgorzelski.

Judy Hoover critiqued chapters, shared her considerable experience of politics, and humored the author.

Kenneth R. Hoover

CONTENTS

Ideology and Political Life

ONE

Ideology is . . . a kind of free creative play of the intellect probing the world. An uneducated Black convict in the United States is no less likely to construct an ideological explanation of his world than a British historian seeking to dramatize the dangers of competition in weapons of destruction. . . . Political scientists use the word to describe any of the more evolved bodies of political doctrine in which theory is combined with a project of political action.

Kenneth Minogue
*Alien Powers: The Pure
Theory of Ideology* (1985)

Introduction

Ideas provide images of the world—images that are used to give shape to our thoughts and feelings. To the extent that they are held in common, these images open up the possibility of shared insights and action. This book is about shared images of a particularly powerful kind: political ideologies.

What are ideologies? Many people think that other people's beliefs are ideological, as if that were bad, but not their own. It is true that not all political beliefs are ideological, but whether or not you yourself have an ideology can better be judged once a general definition of ideology is in hand and you have understood the examples of ideology in this book. In the scholarship of ideology, there are many definitions distinguishing ideology from philosophy, theory, and personal predisposition. To make the concept as accessible as possible, we will take a broad view of ideology.

Generally, an ideology consists of ideas about how power in society should be organized—ideas that are derived from a view of the problems and possibilities inherent in human nature in its individual and social aspects. All ideologies have some sort of characterization of the human condition at their core, even if it is the denial that all people share a common human nature. The characterizations all employ images of power relationships between individuals and society. It is these images that provide the starting point for each chapter. They are the inspiration for the plan of action that each ideology contains.

In the name of conservatism, liberalism, Marxism, fascism, and the other ideologies discussed here, great sacrifices have been made, societies have been reshaped, and wars have been fought. Yet the public understanding of these ideologies has been confused by historical changes, competing interpretations, sloganizing, and deceptive advertising by candidates and political parties. The plan of this book is to describe each image as vividly as possible and then to analyze its origins and meanings.

We will see in each image and analysis the visions of theorists who have shaped the main ideas. What assumptions lie behind the theories? Which assumptions might be open to some kind of evaluation based on observation and experience? What distribution of advantage and deprivation follows from each image?

Most of us can't conceive of living in a society that fits precisely with one or another of these images. Instead, we would find that elements of each ideology are represented among the people and activities of most nations and communities. The conflicts within a society are often shaped by those who are acting on contrasting ideological assumptions. The assumptions may not be clear to the user, and they are often the more potent for being unanalyzed. Our analysis is directed toward untangling these various threads of assumption and argument.

Ideology is a crucial part of political life. Few people will obey (or defy) authority without some kind of justification. Modern societies build huge structures of authority on concepts of power that are derived from ideologies. As we will see, Karl Marx's ideological conceptions provided a justification for revolutions in two of the largest nations in the world. The revolution that established the United States Constitution was deeply influenced by ideologies imported from Europe. Contemporary political discussion centers on the rival claims of liberals and conservatives.

Ideological systems embracing ideas of economics and sociology, politics and philosophy supply the integrating intellectual themes of a culture. They form a language of justification for myriad decisions affecting people's lives together. Whether such ideas really do govern our actions cannot be conclusively determined, but that action is linked to ideas there is no doubt.

To understand an ideology is to see what the ideas about power involve and to understand how they are related to assumptions about the individual and community life. To evaluate an ideology, one must add to this understanding an analysis of whether the assumptions are correct, the linkages to ideas about power are reasonable, and the recipes for governing are workable. This is a tall order. Our purpose here is to enable you to understand and begin to evaluate what is presented these days as ideology.

This book is not a comprehensive history of ideologies. Spokespeople for the various ideologies have been selected from the point of view of one trained in political philosophy. I have tried to single out the most important figures, not necessarily as they were viewed in their own time but rather as they appear from a contemporary perspective. Who contributed most significantly to the ideologies we live with today? As a consequence of this focus, the history will not always be chronological, certainly not encyclopedic, and will omit mention of many who are important in favor of a concentration on those who crystallized the essential changes.

In order to understand the approach taken to ideology in these chapters, one common distinction needs to be undone: that between politics and economics. The title of the book is *Ideology and Political Life;* the phrase "political ideology" does not appear in the title because politics and economics can't be separated from each other at the level of ideology. As succeeding chapters will illustrate, conceptions about power concern economics in a very fundamental sense.

Apart from this approach, there is a larger argument to the book. As the table of contents makes evident, the sequence of chapters proceeds in such a way as to construct a discussion. Classical liberalism is the protagonist in the discussion since our culture is steeped in it. After considering the image of political life sponsored by liberalism, we move to its historical rival: traditional conservatism. The next chapter shows how modern conservatism has been influenced by the classical liberal tradition in the form of libertarian ideology, which is contrasted with anarchism. We move on to discuss "reform" liberalism, the modern face of liberalism. From there, we shift consideration to the major alternatives to liberalism and conservatism: Marxism and socialism. The concluding chapters deal with feminist and minority liberation ideologies and with fascism.

Having established the differences, and perhaps even exploited the distinctions to increase the contrasts, we will try to find in the concluding chapter common characteristics of ideologies and a perspective for working out a personal view of ideology.

This book considers the most sweeping questions of human association. If these ideas meet with your individual experience in revealing ways, and if there be guidance here for well-informed action, then we have accomplished our main purpose.

TWO

The community is a fictitious *body,* composed of the individual persons who are considered as constituting as it
were its *members.* The interest of the community then is,
what?—the sum of the interests of the several members
who compose it.

Jeremy Bentham (1789)

Classical
Liberalism

The liberal image of political life has had a powerful impact. It has permeated Western society and it is the focal point of major critiques from socialists on the left and conservatives on the right. It is easiest to see the liberal image by the use of an illustration. We will construct a liberal utopia: a community with a marketplace and a representative government. As we draw out the implications of this illustration, the liberal concept of politics will become clear.

The hallmark of all truly powerful ideological systems is that they come to be seen as sacred in a religious sense or, in our secular age, as "natural."[1] From this fact arises the difficulty in understanding liberalism: it is so rooted in our culture as to be nearly unconscious. To retrieve the ideas for analysis requires first that we create a simplified and idealized model of the liberal polity. Using that image as a beginning point, we can explore the history and implications of the liberal view of political life.

The notion of a community organized around a representative government and a marketplace is at the core of the liberal image of political life. It is a community of people pursuing their own interests in a context of rules and procedures that maximize personal freedom, with the hoped-for result of social benefit. The structure of power, both political and economic, relates intimately to the functioning of the marketplace. For the moment, we will set aside notions of the separability of economics and politics. Set aside also current meanings of the term *liberal*. The first task is to develop the classical liberal position and, later, its connection to contemporary liberalism and the "welfare state" (see Chapter Five on reform liberalism).

■ The Liberal Image

The liberal community is organized by two basic institutions: the marketplace and representative government. Theoretically, in the perfect market, the jobs would all be performed by those most expert in each specialization. And to the extent that an individual is ambitious, he or she could rise or fall, prosper or languish, according to effort. Access to goods and services is determined by the resources, whether in the form of labor or capital, of each individual. The rise and fall of prices in response to supply and demand sets the framework for consumption. Everyone would presumably benefit from this efficient application of energy and talent to the satisfaction of people's wants.

Informal influence in the community comes largely from people's relation to the marketplace. The owners of land and businesses are widely perceived to occupy a different social and economic standing from that of their clerks, tenants, workers, and wage laborers. To the extent that there is competition within the various economic classes, as well as among them, the market holds the key to individual mobility.

The market has other implications for the life of the community. It sets the major agenda for the political institutions. In order to have an orderly method of rewarding producers for their efforts, there need to be a number of institutions that are protected by a government. Foremost among those institutions is private property. Without the right to own property and to lay claim to the results of labor and of capital investment, there would be—so the liberal thinks—only theft, coercion, and even, as seventeenth century political philosopher Thomas Hobbes put it, "a war of all against all."[2]

The protection of private property and the formulation of laws governing its use and exchange occupy the major part of the lawmaking function that is carried on by the representatives of the people. Proposing and enforcing those laws is the business of the executive, and disputes between property owners are generally settled by the judiciary. Through representative government, individuals and organized interests compete for power by influencing elections and political appointments, pressuring for legislation, and shaping law enforcement practices.

Contracts enforced by the state are the legal means for the maintenance of property relationships, including marriage. Contractual relations replace personal associations as the institutions of private property and the marketplace come to dominate community life.

Politics is shaped in other ways by the market. Good facilities for commercial development are desirable, and thus attention is given to roads, utilities, industrial areas, and so forth. These facilities form the infrastructure for trade. Education to provide the skills necessary for competition in the marketplace becomes a major concern of the government.

As the market occupies the center of economic, social, and political life, it creates a competitive ethos generally. Just as competition is institutionalized as the key to survival, people become used to competing in other aspects of their existence. Rational procedures for conducting competition become the objective of legislation and the centerpiece of hiring and advancement policies.

The intellectual justification for classical liberalism grows out of an image of the fullest possible freedom for individual belief, expression, and production. It is through the ideal of freedom of expression that the dignity of the individual is upheld. Freedom is viewed as maximizing personal choice over the widest possible range of expression and consumption. Intellectual freedom is justified as competition in the "marketplace" of ideas.

Just as the theoretical conception of freedom is associated with the notion of the marketplace, restrictions on freedom emerge from the need to limit one particular sort of behavior: interference by one individual with the rights and property of another. To deny another person the same freedom of expression and material accumulation we wish to have for ourselves is contrary to the good of the community. Similarly, to use government to foreclose people's choices of religion, occupation, beliefs, or interests is considered unjust if it cannot be justified by identifying some overriding threat to public safety.[3]

If we had been designing the government for a liberal utopia at the end of the eighteenth century, we would have reproduced many elements of the U.S. Constitution. There would be executive, legislative, and judicial branches of government and the familiar ritual of elections, fixed terms of office, and legal restraints on the power of officials. Less familiar would be the restrictions on who could vote for and serve in public office. In 1789, suffrage was limited largely to white male property owners over the age of 21. Slaves were counted as inferior beings and their status as property was temporarily acknowledged in the U.S. Constitution. Since government existed to protect property and the framework of the marketplace, there was thought to be no point in enfranchising or empowering people who did not have a settled economic interest in the system.

Little by little through the last two centuries, the system has become more democratic. We now have a version of liberalism that combines the marketplace with representative government on the basis of nearly universal suffrage. The system was democratized because of the struggles of those previously excluded from participating. Throughout these struggles, the argument for democracy was always the immortal proposition that "all men are created equal"—an argument based on faith in the Creator rather than the marketplace. Yet it took the development of economic power by the working class, by minorities, and by women to force the issue of participation against the resistance of entrenched interests based on property and white male preeminence. More recently, democratization resulted from crises in the system that have made demands on all sectors of the population: women in the era of the First World War, blacks in the Second World War, eighteen-year-olds in the Vietnam War. Having been called upon to help the nation in a time of crisis, they weren't interested in being excluded from access to representative institutions.

So the marketplace creates the system of preferment and status, sets an agenda for the functions of government, and influences the style and character of personal life. This powerful image of free people interacting through a marketplace and representative government, while perfecting their individual talents, is at the heart of the classical liberal view of political life.

A contemporary liberal theorist, John Rawls, has modernized this imagery by using the metaphor of a game rather than a marketplace. Organized games allow each person to make the most of his or her position within a framework that will assign results to people's behavior. That's why games have rules, referees, and scores. If everyone plays his or her part well, a good play of the game is achieved and rewards are distributed in accordance with some worthy principle such as effort or the best exercise of a talent.[4]

To return from a modern to a classical analysis, the reasoning behind the liberal image of politics can be most clearly seen in what appears as a purely economic version of it. In a famous passage, Adam Smith in *The Wealth of Nations* (1776) argues that if every person uses his or her assets so as to maximize economic return,

> every individual necessarily labours to render the annual revenue of the society as great as he can. He generally, indeed, neither intends to promote the public interest, nor knows how much he is promoting it . . . he intends only his own gain, and he is in this, as in many other cases, led by an invisible hand to promote an end which was no part of his intention."[5]

Although Adam Smith was not addressing politics directly in this paragraph, he set the tone for many liberal theorists who see politics as a derivative of some other human activity. That activity is the pursuit of self-interest. The image of the liberal polity revolves around the notion that each person will, by developing his or her own interests and abilities, yield for others the necessities and amenities that will make their lives better. The function of government is mainly to assure that people have the freedom to engage in this pursuit.[6]

The rhetoric of liberalism, with its emphasis on individuality, freedom, and economic development, is very attractive to the modern mind. In order to analyze its origins and see how it has been criticized, we need to understand its history.

■ Analyzing the Origins of Liberalism

The fundamental theme of liberalism is the freedom of the individual. For the purposes of understanding the ideology, we can establish a sequence of three ways that individual freedom has been justified. There is a rough sort of progression from one mode of justification to the next. The first mode rests on the tradition of *natural law*, the second on the concept of *individualism*, and the third on a theory of *self-interest*. Each set of arguments will be considered as we develop an understanding of classical liberalism.

Liberalism and Natural Law

The history of conceptions of natural law is tangled and rich. Our plan is to make sense of it by concentrating on an emerging theme: the notion that the individual is at the center of God's rational order. This concept, which we may call *natural individualism*, constitutes the earliest version of liberalism. After exploring this development, we will see briefly how the transition was effected to the more modern liberal notion of self-interest as a basis for political life.

What is natural law? It can be seen most clearly in Christian political thought. The argument is that the world we live in has an inherent structure; it is organized around certain general principles. The political theory of Christianity from the beginning to the present is little else than an exploration of man's relation to a divinely created natural order. With the possible exception of Ecclesiastes in the Old Testament, no Judeo-Christian theologian ever argued that God's world is random. It is the conception of natural order that gives religion its power to resolve the doubts and uncertainties of the faithful. The major issue in Christian political philosophy was not whether there was order or chaos but rather how the order could be understood.

Medieval Christians thought that natural law could be known only through devotion, prayer, and self-purification. Monasteries and nunneries were designed to make those practices possible. In the deceptively mild words of St. Augustine, we could understand God's natural order only by entering into His "community of love."

But what Augustine meant by love was the simple recognition that order could be achieved only in heaven and that our best course of action on earth was submission to authority. This is the Christian concept of order at its most politically remote.

Christian theologians finally came to rationalism in their search for a way of understanding God's natural order. In the thirteenth century, Thomas Aquinas (1225–1274), borrowing from Aristotle, put forward reason as the tool that could be used to uncover the meaning of God's plan. It was the legitimation of human reason, rather than blind faith and tradition, as a guide for behavior that was the liberal element in Aquinas's thought. The alliance of reason with religion was an extraordinarily bold stroke.

It is not far from baptizing reason to confirming individualism. If reason can unlock the secrets of the natural order, and if reason is found in all individuals, then the possibility exists of placing human judgment at the center of politics. This argument opens the way for the construction of a political order around the exercise of individual reason, rather than the approximation of a divine plan interpreted by priests and kings.

Nevertheless, Aquinas's direct thought on politics was hardly liberal. He quotes approvingly the traditional maxim that "the good of the nation is more godlike than the good of one man."[7] It is the function of human law not to express human perceptions but to approximate natural and divine laws.

What was riding on the outcome of the debate about the intelligibility of natural law was, quite simply, power. If natural law is sacred and mysterious, and human beings are the helpless creatures of a divine master, then there can be no politics in the conscious sense, for there are no real choices to be made. Power then belongs to religiously sanctioned authority and is not accountable to human judgment.

If, on the other hand, every citizen can potentially understand and interpret natural law, then the construction of a political community becomes a most absorbing and demanding task. Power becomes accountable to human judgment, and power can be shared among the members of the community who understand the natural order.

From Natural Law to Natural Individualism

Two steps lay between medieval Christian thought and the development of a liberal individualist theory based on natural law. First, the individual had to acquire a significance equal to or greater than that of the society as a whole. Second, an argument had to be developed that would endow this newly discovered individual with a unique and distinctive role to play in the natural order of things.

The first of these tasks was performed with revolutionary consequences by Martin Luther (1483–1546), John Calvin (1509–1564), and the Protestant reformers. It was they who challenged the notion of a spiritual and secular order dominated by the Roman Catholic Church. It was the Protestant Reformation that put the individual into a private relationship with God. The individual, having been recognized as the center of religious concern, soon became the focus of political thought.

The Protestant reformers fueled the revolt, but the struggle against the traditional order was carried in the end by an audacious band of eighteenth century French political theorists. It was their ambitious project to make human reason itself divine.[8] Rather than seeing human attempts at rationality as poor imitations of the Divine, the Enlightenment theorists located the divine principle in the mind of the reasonable man. Once they had done so, religion became irrelevant to politics. For the Baron de Montesquieu (1689–1755), government could be based on secular authority and controlled through checking and balancing powers among different branches—an idea that found its way directly into the U.S. Constitution. In the French Revolution of 1789, the notion of a natural order based on reason was turned around and used against the clergy and the authority of the church. They were consigned to the dust heap of archaic institutions whose basis in tradition and custom was ridiculed as irrational and authoritarian.

The building of a polity became an exercise in deduction from the universal principles of a rational human nature. As Carl Becker remarked in *The Heavenly City of the Eighteenth Century Philosophers,*

> What these "universal principles" were the Philosophers, therefore, understood before they went in search of them, and with "man in general" they were well acquainted, having created him in their own image. They knew instinctively that "man in general" is natively good, easily enlightened, disposed to follow reason and common sense; generous and humane and tolerant, more easily led by persuasion than compelled by force; above all a good citizen and a man of virtue, being well aware that, since the rights claimed by himself are only the natural and imprescriptible rights of all men, it is necessary for him voluntarily to assume the obligations and to submit to the restraints imposed by a just government for the commonweal.[9]

Given this principled citizen, statecraft was no great mystery. The political machinery could be designed as if it were clockwork, though the French revolution of 1789 moved more frequently to the metronomic rhythm of the guillotine as real and suspected enemies of the new order were publicly beheaded.

The Protestant Reformation provided the justification for a new individualism, while the French *philosophes* and their English liberal allies, whom we shall soon introduce, endowed the individual with reason. The cause of individualism was to receive a powerful assist from a student of the French and English rationalists, Thomas Jefferson (1743–1826). As befits someone who made his living on the land rather than in the city, Jefferson's assertion of the primacy of the individual was based on the ability of the individual to play a particular role in the divine order of things—a role that can be acted out only by the assertion of our individual talents and abilities. Jefferson was impressed with the natural order in a direct sense.

Jefferson saw himself as a "natural scientist" of society. If the Divine Creator intends each individual to be unique, then to carry through on that distinctiveness is the natural mission of each individual. Just as we derive our equality from an "equal creation," so we derive our unique creaturehood from the same source. Thus the free expression of one's individuality is not a privilege to be granted by the polity but a right based in nature. In Jefferson's hands, liberalism became a theory dedicated to the guarantee of equal rights and freedom of expression, for these were the conditions by which the divinity in man could come to the surface and be displayed to the advantage of the community.

This view may sound like a recipe for anarchism, with individuals heading off in all sorts of contrary directions and political community left stranded at the crossroads. Yet Jefferson believed in a kind of discipline that links individuals to a larger order. As Daniel Boorstin suggests, "The proper test, the Jeffersonian declared, was not what a man believed, but how accurately and honestly he avowed whatever the Creator had destined him to believe. The ideas which a man professed were less important than whether these ideas were the characteristic expression of the mind which the Creator had given him."[10] To put it simply, in diversity there is divinity.

The connection between creaturehood and polity, Jefferson thought, could only be explained by God's design, for, after all, "The Creator would indeed have been a bungling artist, had he intended man for a social animal, without planting in him social dispositions."[11] Creaturehood is in the last analysis a concept distinct from individuality. Because we are created beings, in Jefferson's view, our interpersonal variations are the measure not of our distance from others but of our complementarity in a larger natural cosmos. Jefferson places us as a species among other life forms having deep and abiding common ties.

The Jeffersonian conception of natural liberty as both the design of God and the fulfillment of an enlightened view of human nature united two powerful streams of thought: the sacred and the secular versions of individualism. God was responsible for our individuality, but it is up to each of us to act out our particular role in the social order. Jefferson's view of liberty remains in our vocabulary and rhetoric and occasionally in our jurisprudence. Indeed it may be the only effective intellectual barrier we have to the total domination of our culture by the structure of power emanating from the marketplace. Yet it is the latter, with its roots in a quite different tradition of political argument, that has become the major theme of classical liberalism.

The Liberalism of Self-Interest

The movement toward an argument for natural liberty was superseded by an even more powerful rival: liberty based on a conception of self-interest. As we shall see, it makes a great deal of difference whether liberty is justified as a natural endowment of the Creator or as an accommodation of our appetites and interests.

For political theory, the debate over nature versus interest is exceedingly consequential. If the political community is no more than the sum of the property relations of individuals, then all we need to know about politics may be studied in the form of zoning arrangements, tax rates, and police services. Many people have this idea of their political life. But if a polity is something more, a natural expression of a need in human life, with a complex of sociological, psychological, and cultural functions to perform, then politics is far more diverse and varied.

To understand this debate between nature and self-interest better, it is important to consider how it began. In the beginning, the concept of interest was the child of natural law, and the child grew to overwhelm the parent. Let us see how this happened.[12]

The concept originated as the idea that the society had an interest paramount to that of the individual. The interest of the society was defined quite simply as order. Drawing on the medieval Christian fear of the anarchy that uncontrolled passion releases, and using the evidence of the brutalities of politics in the age of the Borgias and the Medicis (remember Romeo and Juliet?), Niccolo Machiavelli (1469–1527) could make the establishment of order the most important political value without having to argue very hard for it. If, as seemed to be the case, order could be produced only in a well-led state, then it was easy to justify all means necessary for the achievement of that end. In such a climate of moral relativism was the concept of interest born.

Interest as the organizing principle gained wherever the feudal order lost. Interest was the concept of the traders, the city-dwellers, the merchants, and that restless force in European history, the newly emergent middle class. It superseded *virtue*, which was the concept of theologians intent on controlling human vice. The attempt to constrain the vices through the elaboration of an order based on fealty and honor, the church and chivalry, gave way in time to a more energetic, mobile, and commercial culture organized around the nation-state.

What follows upon Machiavelli's formulation of the concept of interest is a series of modifications, first from national interest to the notion of group interest, then to individual interest, and finally to economic self-interest. These transformations were largely the work of seventeenth century English liberals.

From Group Interest to Self-Interest: The Rise of English Liberalism

Thomas Hobbes (1588–1679), who stands at the beginning of the English liberal line of thought, ridiculed the tender notions of medieval feudalism, with its stations and classes, religious piety, network of obligations and duties, and overarching imagery of harmony and natural order. He spoke instead of the authority of the state in the imagery of a "Leviathan" who "hath the use of so much Power and Strength conferred on him, that by terror thereof, he is enabled to forme the wills of them all, to Peace at home, and mutuall ayd against their enemies abroad." In this Leviathan, declared Hobbes, "consisteth the Essence of the Commonwealth," and in the absence of such power, "men have no pleasure, (but on the contrary a great deale of griefe) in keeping company."[13] So much for community life in any but the most artificial sense.

The basis for this extreme position was a new view of the meaning of life based solely and completely on the radical notion of individualism. It was this question of raw survival in the jungle of individual competition that melded personal appetites into a united and powerful group interest sufficient to justify extreme forms of authority.

Hobbes located the mainspring of human nature in appetite; John Locke (1632–1704), agreeing with his major premise, emphasized the crucial observation that people are rational. Their rationality provides the possibility of a community based on something a bit more ambitious than mere survival: an active interest in "the regulating and preserving of property."[14]

Locke sees us as having the capacity to understand our interests and to regulate our interactions with others, whereas Hobbes allows only the abandonment of authority over a crucial part of our lives in the hope to obtain thereby the "preservation" of life and property. It is this notion of regulation that transforms Locke's system into a true theory of political community. Locke frequently refers, as Hobbes does not, to community as a synonym for government.

Locke recommends a two-phase political construction. The society is based on a *contract;* the government is based on a *trust.* The contract brings individuals together for the purpose of settling disputes: "*the community comes to be umpire,* by settled standing rules; indifferent and the same to all parties."[15] So long as the society serves the purpose of regulating and preserving property, the contract can't be revoked. For the purpose of making this contract a reality, a government is created by the members of the society and entrusted with appropriate powers. It is to establish clear and specific laws, set up judges to settle conflicts, and supply the force necessary to penalize those who violate the law. The government stays in power according to the terms established for it and with the understanding that it will not exceed the purposes of its formation. Thus, regulation occurs within the polity.

Locke modified Hobbes's simple ideas of fear and instinct by centering his theory on people's rational interest in the protection of property. This interest becomes the basis for a political order. Locke declared,

> Political power, then, I take to be a right of making laws, with penalties of death, and consequently all less penalties, for the regulating and preserving of property, and of employing the force of the community, in the execution of such laws, and in the defense of the commonwealth from foreign injury, and all this only for the public good.[16]

Note that Locke, like Smith, identifies the public good with the proper ordering of economic activity.

Hobbes and Locke both appreciated the need for a sphere of personal belief that was to be protected and set apart from the power of the state. However, to set matters of conscience outside the power of the state is to consign them to irrelevance when it comes to the main business of the community, which is, precisely, business. It is this arrangement that gives to liberal communities their amoral aspect. English liberalism has to do with ensuring freedom of choice in the acquisition and disposition of property, not with enacting a particular morality.

The Impact of English Liberalism on Politics

Thomas Hobbes saw no particular rationality in the claims of one person as against another. Hobbes makes the point absolutely clear: "To this warre of every man against every man, this also is consequent: that nothing can be unjust. The notions of right and wrong, justice and injustice have there no place. Where there is no common power, there is no law: where no law, no injustice."[17] Thus, Hobbes's solution was force exercised in the name of the people, whereas Locke's rationalist solution tends more toward regulation and adjudication. The institutionalized performance of these functions separates a political society from the state of nature.

In legitimizing the concept of individual interest, Locke gave it a broad definition: the interest that draws individuals together is "the mutual preservation of their lives, liberties, and estates which I call by the general name, property."[18] In this capacious definition there is room for a fairly wide range of community concerns. Following upon a Lockean design, our own Constitution gives to Congress the generous mandate to make laws to "provide for the common defense and to promote the general welfare of the United States." The point is that, although Locke developed a theory of limited government responsive to the people, he conceived of the functions that the people might delegate to the government as substantial and wide-ranging.[19]

Locke's broad-based rationalist conception of the nature of individual self-interest gave new hope to those who continued to look for a solution to the old problem of controlling human vice. If an interest in "our lives, our fortunes, and our sacred honor" could be made the central principle of social organization, then there might be a recipe for order that would tie us together in a durable social contract. Yet some critics thought that self-interest might be another name for avarice. However, the apologists of property were ready with two arguments: that commerce based upon property would induce order in the society, as well as discipline in individuals through their citizenship in the state. These results would compensate for whatever concessions were made to avarice and greed.

David Hume (1711–1776), a Scottish philosopher, spoke for this whole movement when he said, "It is an infallible consequence of all industrious professions, to . . . make the love of gain prevail over the love of pleasure."[20] If virtue is the end result, goes the argument, then the means to that end must be virtuous by implication. In this case, the means to the end are the pursuit of individual interest.

Now the outlines of a liberal utopia are beginning to emerge. So influential has Locke been that Louis Hartz in *The Liberal Tradition in America* could argue that the popular doctrine of "the American way of life" is nothing more than a "nationalist articulation of Locke."[21] Although other scholars disagree and cite important elements of traditionalism and natural law in the Constitution, there is no question that Locke was a major influence on our notions of contract, consent, and property.[22]

Self-Interest and the Marketplace

The theme of this section has been the attempt to bring interest into the battle against the disorderly tendencies of human nature, and so to establish a benign polity. Machiavelli, Hobbes, and Locke all rely upon variations of this formula in their theories of politics. We have come now to the point of confrontation with the latent conflict between interest and vice. As Albert Hirschman tells it in *The Passions and the Interests: Political Arguments for Capitalism before Its Triumph,* it was Adam Smith who reengineered the argument into its most compelling form. It was indeed arguable whether the interest in property could control such vices as avarice or whether interest was in fact avarice by another name. For Smith, the problem was resolved by a simple and powerful reduction of the terms of the controversy.

Smith argues that the passions of lust, ambition, and vainglory, those durable villains of medieval religious thought, are in fact reducible to a single passion: vanity. It is preferment in the eyes of others that draws together all our activity, according to Smith: "To be observed, to be attended to, to be taken notice of with sympathy, complacency, and appreciation are all the advantages which we can propose to derive from it. It is the vanity, not the ease or the pleasure, which interests us."[23]

Rather than falling victim to a contest among the passions, then, we have only to learn how to harness the one grand passion, namely vanity, to the service of order and we shall have resolved the central problem of political thought. Smith removes the opposition between interest and vice. He says that the pursuit of vanity, in the properly organized society, can work to the advantage of all. It is vanity, captured and directed by the marketplace into productive activity, that is, paradoxically, to save us from our passionate selves. Commerce reduces passion to interest. By this device, Smith is able to believe in the fallibility of human nature and a sort of material perfectibility of society simultaneously!

After Smith, the political community as the center of shared values, mutuality, and the means for the development and sustenance of human life dissolves into the marketplace and the rule of supply and demand. The polity, then, has no intrinsic function or worth; it is merely the aggregation of rationalized functions related to the disciplined pursuit of vanity.

For Smith, the meaning of one's self-interest is defined not by individual talents and abilities, as Jefferson has it, or by every human being's natural desire to obtain and secure the means of subsistence, as Locke proposes, but by whatever commerce commands and ambition allows. Smith deprives individual life of all attachment to a natural order or to any kind of deeper meaning. He may as well have quoted Hobbes: "The *value*, or worth of a man, is as of all other things, his price; that is to say, so much as would be given for the use of his power. . . ."[24]

The difference is that in such anarchy, Hobbes recognizes the need for absolute order imposed by the state, else there would be "a war of all against all." Smith assumes that the market will generate its own order. In Smith's analysis, the force that keeps order is concealed behind an economic vocabulary of prices, supply, demand, and marginal costs. What illegitimate force is exerted through theft and violence as a corollary of the inequalities produced by the market is not accounted for in the carefully ruled ledger of the economist.

Back to Politics: Utilitarian Liberalism

We have seen how Smith summarized all passion as vanity and reduced it to economic self-interest through the institution of the marketplace. Some of this doctrine's implications for politics have been explored. However, the more explicitly political dimension of utilitarianism was formulated by Smith's younger contemporary, Jeremy Bentham. It was Bentham's radical proposal that self-interest be defined in even less discriminating fashion. Bentham declared:

> Nature has placed mankind under the governance of two sovereign masters, *pain* and *pleasure*. It is for them alone to point out what we ought to do, as well as to determine what we shall do. On the one hand the standard of right and wrong, on the other, the chain of causes and effects are fastened to their throne.[25]

From this observation, he deduced the famous principle of utility, which is to guide the judgment of each action by the "tendency which it appears to have to augment or diminish the happiness of the party whose interest is in question. . . ."[26] Bentham allows that pains and pleasures are simply "interesting perceptions."[27] What Smith begins when he reduces motivation to the single indiscriminate notion of vanity, Bentham finishes by casting individual self-interest in a form so general that it defies all but the most rudimentary classification.

Yet politics is about the making of decisions, so interest does have to be defined in particular cases. That process of judgment, Bentham implies, must be placed in the hands of the people. Since there can be no general definition of pleasure and pain that holds for all individuals, a representative government must play the crucial role of summarizing the utilitarian calculations of all individuals. The society will then be guided by the principle of "the greatest happiness of the greatest number."

In his time, Bentham was seen as a great reformer and spent much of his life working on proposals for modernizing Britain's antiquated penal system. He is the author of the notion that punishment for crime should be calculated to dissuade potential criminals and to reform those who are caught rather than to punish them for their "sins." The great project of his life was the reform of the English legal code so that it would administer pain in such a way as to "place every member of political society in such circumstances that his private interest might coincide with the general interest."[28] He worked to purge religious conceptions from their role in public law.

What Bentham initiates is the ultimate democratization of liberalism. No longer does power have to be linked to a defined sphere of activity for "the protection of life, liberty, and estate," as in Locke. Public power may be deployed however the population wishes. Bentham intended to free society from the shackles of tradition, custom, and privilege; while he was at it he freed politics of all boundaries, morality of all content, and community of all meaning save the collective pursuit of pleasure by whatever definition its current residents might have.

Second Thoughts: Utilitarian Liberalism Modified

The long battle to free individuals from the yoke of traditional power and privilege acquired, by virtue of the work of Bentham and Smith, a powerful new theory. The simplicity of the pleasure-pain calculation opened the way to the reform of English politics and made utilitarianism the favorite theory of many men and women of progressive views. The institutional inventions of Smith and Bentham have merited careful attention here because the arguments they generated are still with us in the works of such contemporary theorists as Milton Friedman who have influenced present-day politics[29] (see Chapter Four on libertarian conservatism).

As the implications of utilitarian liberalism began to reverberate through English society, critics were quick to see that all pleasures might come out equal on the public scales and anarchism (or despotism) could be the result. In addition, the proposal for so radical a form of democratic representative government offered the prospect of the blind leading the blind on serious questions of public policy. It was up to John Stuart Mill to rescue liberalism from these difficulties. In doing so, he revitalized the movement but changed some of its most basic assumptions.

John Stuart Mill (1806–1873) attempted to save utilitarianism from the accusation that it fostered a mindless materialism. He did this by developing two powerful arguments. The first was that society must pursue not just the sum of individual interests understood at any given moment but rather the formation of rules that would serve for all individuals in similar situations. Although a temporary majority may decide that it would take great pleasure in eliminating people with green eyes, the act of doing so would open up all other subgroups to threats of extermination and society would descend into chaos. So, by Mill's *rule* utilitarianism (as opposed to *act* utilitarianism), no minority should ever be targeted for prejudicial treatment. This principle, applied to all policy questions, was intended to restrain the power of the majority to do as it wished.

The principle of rule utilitarianism can be institutionalized through constitutional protections and by the election of wise people to public office—a point that brings up Mill's other major contribution to the revision of liberalism. Early utilitarians had seemed to argue that any person is as good a judge of pleasure and pain as any other. That principle appears to follow from the radically individualist assumptions Bentham proclaimed. But Mill pointed out that if all human beings learn through experience, then some have more experience than others. We should entrust decisions to those who are the most experienced. Thus Mill introduces an element of elitism into liberalism.

Mill limits the power of the majority, and of the elite, in another way, however. In his famous defense of civil liberties, *On Liberty*, Mill argues that whereas some may have more experience in making decisions than others, no one knows for certain the whole truth about anything. It follows that free expression should always be protected, even from majority censure, since we can never be sure that any person's ideas are entirely without merit. This classic argument has inspired more than a century of struggle for freedom of expression.

In attempting to save utilitarianism from its critics, Mill changed some of its key propositions. He both made overtures to democratic socialism and opened up classical liberalism to challenges of a more sweeping character that will be dealt with later. However, one more version of liberalism needs to be reviewed before the picture begins to be complete. In the late nineteenth century, under the influence of Georg Friedrich Hegel (1770–1831), liberalism took a new form based not in experience, appetite, and interest but in the nature of the mind.

Thomas Hill Green (1836–1882), an English interpreter of Hegel, proposed a theory called liberal idealism. Green believed that what was missing in utilitarianism was any argument that brought individuals of differing interests into a true community. Green's study of Hegel convinced him that all individuals share a common structure of intellect through the power of reasoning. We all are capable of perceiving, with appropriate thought and education, the same principles of justice because they are embedded in the mind. On the basis of this common structure, people can build a polity that realizes the inherent principles of justice appropriate to a humane existence.

The search for these inherent principles of justice proved to be challenging. Liberal idealists, powerful politically at the turn of the twentieth century, had a hard time stating clearly the exact content of their ideas. Nevertheless, liberal idealism represented another advance for arguments of individualism, equality, and reason. What was new was the added significance assigned to political community as the arbiter not merely of interest but of justice. In this respect, T. H. Green was a transitional thinker to modern reform liberalism.

For all the power of these ideas, it was the advent of the industrial revolution that speeded the implementation of classical liberalism. In an age of entrepreneurs, shopkeepers, and newly independent workers, the concept of individual self-interest fit neatly into the experience of the times. As the full consequences of individual self-interest in an era of economic boom and bust became apparent, the foundations of classical liberalism came under increasingly critical scrutiny.[30]

■ *Conclusion*

Both the later Mill, who begins to be skeptical of the materialism of the market-based society, and the idealist Thomas Hill Green led liberalism away from its classical foundations. John Stuart Mill, toward the end of his life, made overtures to a democratic form of socialism. The search by Green and others for principles of justice fueled a reform movement in England that found its echo in American progressivism. We will see how the problems they tried to address entered into the formation of reform liberalism in the United States.

The formulation of classical liberalism as the combination of a marketplace and a representative government became the principal force in reshaping political thought, and with it the design and operation of political systems in many parts of the world. This powerful idea system is not without its challengers then or now. The remainder of our study of political thought will focus on the ways that classical liberalism has been confronted by alternative ideologies.

We have become accustomed to hearing that the defense of the marketplace is a conservative position. We will see how that association developed in Chapter Four on libertarian conservatism. In Chapter Five, the story of how liberals came to believe in governmental intervention in the economy is told. But before that, it is important to understand the position of classical liberalism's historical rival, traditional conservatism.

■ *Notes*

[1]For detailed interpretations of the rise of classical liberalism, see Karl Polanyi, *The Great Transformation: The Political and Economic Origins of Our Time* (Boston: Beacon Press, 1957), and Louis Dumont, *From Mandeville to Marx: The Genesis and Triumph of Economic Ideology* (Chicago: University of Chicago Press, 1977).

[2]For the history of this line of development in classical liberalism, see C. B. Macpherson, *The Political Theory of Possessive Individualism* (New York: Oxford University Press, 1962), and the extension of this analysis to contemporary politics in Macpherson's *The Real World of Democracy* (New York: Oxford University Press, 1966).

[3]For a summary of some of the nuances in the discussion of "Kantian" and "Millsian" approaches to classical liberalism, see Michael Sandel, *Liberalism and the Limits of Justice* (Cambridge: Cambridge University Press, 1982), pp. 1–14.

[4]John Rawls, *A Theory of Justice*, (Cambridge, Mass.: Harvard University Press, 1971), pp. 525–526. What separates games from life is that chance is often used, as in a card game, to randomize the starting position of all players so that everyone may have the possibility of winning.

[5]Adam Smith, *The Wealth of Nations* (New York: Modern Library, 1937), p. 423. Smith continues, "Nor is it always the worse for the society that it was no part of it. By pursuing his own interest he frequently promotes that of the society more effectually than when he really intends to promote it. I have never known much good done by those who affected to trade for the public good. It is an affectation, indeed, not very common among merchants, and very few words need be employed in dissuading them from it."

[6]For a contemporary defense of liberalism, see David Spitz, *The Real World of Liberalism* (Chicago: University of Chicago Press, 1982), especially his liberal "credo," pp. 213–216.

[7]*Political Ideas of St. Thomas Aquinas*, Dino Bigongiari, ed. (New York: Norton, 1953), p. 84.

[8]See Kingsley Martin, *The Rise of French Liberal Thought: A Study of Political Ideas from Bayle to Condorcet*, 2nd ed., ed. by J. P. Mayer (Greenwood Press, 1980, 1954).

[9]Carl Becker, *The Heavenly City of the Eighteenth Century Philosophers* (New Haven: Yale University Press, 1932), p. 103.

[10]Daniel Boorstin, *The Lost World of Thomas Jefferson* (Boston: Beacon Press, 1948), p. 122.

[11]Cited in Garry Wills, *Inventing America: Jefferson's Declaration of Independence* (New York: Vintage, 1978), p. 187.

[12]For a thoughtful study of these developments, see Albert Hirschman, *The Passions and the Interests: Political Arguments for Capitalism before Its Triumph*, (Princeton, N.J.: Princeton University Press, 1977).

[13]Thomas Hobbes, *Leviathan*, edited and introduced by C. B. Macpherson (Baltimore, Md.: Penguin Books, 1968), pp. 227–228, 185.

[14]In Sir Ernest Barker, *Social Contract: Essays by Locke, Hume, and Rousseau* (London: Oxford University Press, 1960), pp. 27–28.

[15]Ibid., p. 50.

[16]Ibid., p. 4.

[17]Hobbes, op. cit., p. 188.

[18]Barker, op. cit., p. 73.

[19]Classical liberalism did, in fact, grow in correspondence with democratic socialist ideas. The fork in the road really came in the work of Adam Smith (1723–1790) and Jeremy Bentham (1748–1832). Smith narrowed the concept of self-interest, and Bentham replaced the tendencies toward mutuality in Lockean thought with radical individualism. Jean Jacques Rousseau (1712–1778), on the other hand, thought that individual self-interest was the problem, not the solution. He concentrated on defining the kind of political environment in which an individual would follow the "general will" rather than private interest.

[20]Cited in Hirschman, *The Passions and the Interests*, p. 66.

[21]Louis Hartz, *The Liberal Tradition in America: An Interpretation of American Political Thought since the Revolution* (New York: Harcourt, 1962), p. 11; for a contrasting view, see Staughton Lynd, *The Intellectual Origins of American Radicalism* (Cambridge, Mass.: Harvard University Press, 1982, 1968).

[22]See, for example, J. G. A. Pocock, ed., *Three British Revolutions* (Princeton, N.J.: Princeton University Press, 1980), pp. 265–289. On the variety of influences on American thinking in this period, see Donald Lutz, "The Relative Influence of European Writers on Late Eighteenth Century American Thought," *The American Political Science Review* 78 (1984):189–197.

[23]In Hirschman, op. cit., p. 108.

[24]Hobbes, op. cit., p. 151.

[25]Jeremy Bentham, "An Introduction to the Principles of Morals and Legislation," in *The Utilitarians* (New York: Doubleday, 1961), p. 17.

[26]Ibid.

[27]Ibid., p. 41.

[28]Guido DeRuggiero, *The History of European Liberalism*, R. C. Collingwood, trans. (London: Oxford University Press, 1927), p. 103.

[29]See Milton Friedman, *Capitalism and Freedom* (Chicago: University of Chicago Press, 1981).

[30]For an interesting anthropological approach to relations of property and contract, see Lewis Hyde, *The Gift: Imagination and the Erotic Life of Property* (New York: Vintage, 1983), especially Chaps. 2, 5, 6.

THREE

[Conservatism] denies the existence of any irreconcilable antagonisms in a healthy body politic. It holds, on the contrary, that the efficiency and prosperity of each class— upper, middle, lower, each with its countless internal gradations—is essential for the wellbeing of the community as a whole. It recognizes the distinction between the classes as natural, fundamental, and beneficial; the same sort of distinction as exists between the head, the body, and the limbs of a man or an animal. But it regards the distinction as one of function mainly, and not necessarily one of honour or emolument.

F. J. C. Hearnshaw (1933)

Traditional Conservatism

As is the case with classical liberalism and reform liberalism, there are differences between the historical meaning of conservatism and its contemporary version. Conservatism became politically significant in the eighteenth and nineteenth centuries as a position based on arguments in favor of the role of tradition and legitimate authority in the polity. This traditionalist view, muted in contemporary conservative thought, was largely overtaken in the last thirty years by a position that we will identify as libertarian conservatism (see Chapter Four). In the context of an acceptance of the inequality of individuals, which libertarians and traditionalists share, there are sharp divergences over the uses and limits of authority. The tensions within modern conservatism can't be understood fully without a knowledge of both the traditionalist and libertarian versions.

The traditional conservative image of political life begins from a view of the human condition that is strikingly different from the liberal conception. Where liberals see the rational individual capable of contracting with others for the mutual improvement of their lives and fortunes, the conservative sees a spiritual, fallible, limited, semirational personality whose behavior cannot be perfected. Rather than using the state to move such creatures toward procedural equality and abstract justice, conservatives concentrate on establishing social and political institutions that will bring out the strengths and minimize the weaknesses in each distinctive personality.[1]

When the traditional conservative looks at the mass of human activity that constitutes political life and asks what gives it order, he or she is most likely to answer that it is leaders and institutions, private and public. Whereas the liberal sees individuals bound together only by an instrumental politics of property and individual rights, the conservative sees society as a web of particular arrangements, authorities, and beliefs arising out of habit, the differences in abilities, and the limitations on human rationality. For the traditionalist conservative, the role of the polity is primary—it is not there merely to accommodate self-interested individuals. The polity serves as the framework for the institutions, customs, ethics, and traditions by which personality is developed and order is maintained.

■ *The Traditionalist Image of Political Life*

For each of life's functions, there are traditional institutions: the family, the church, government, corporations, schools and universities, craft unions, and private associations of all kinds. The conservative view of each of these institutions reveals something about the structure of the traditionalist view of political life.

Personal character is a key consideration. Rather than focusing on individuals as self-interested reasoning machines, conservatives observe that people spend their lives struggling with great forces of temptation. The traditional vices, the pursuit of pleasure rather than duty, the errors of egotism and self-indulgence are what confront us on a daily basis, and they can be overcome only through discipline, faith, and institutional constraints. This view of the human condition has many political implications. However, the basic line of defense against such weaknesses is *character*. The purpose of such institutions as the family, religion, and government is to instill a sense of personal discipline, courage, and motivation. The other functions of these institutions are to deal with the mistakes that people make.

The family has as its prime goal the nurturance of personality and the development of character. The differentiation of roles in the family follows from the need for physical, emotional, and intellectual growth as well as economic sustenance. For each person to play all these roles is to invite incompetence and disorganization. Many conservatives see this differentiation of roles as biologically determined, with the husband as provider and the wife as nurturer. Each has distinctive responsibilities that are essential to the well-being of the whole family.

In some traditionalist writing, the family becomes the metaphor for larger relations of authority. Familial imagery is often a part of conservative writing on government. Just as father, mother, and children have specific roles to play in the family, so do workers, managers, and leaders have roles to play in the proper operation of the society. A disordered society is one in which people move out of their roles without adequate background and preparation.

The church exists not so much to provide a forum for the expression of private notions of spirituality as to furnish a link between people's spiritual inclinations and a larger order through faith in God. Traditionalists are skeptical of tidy schemes for salvation or justice and carry that skepticism into their attitude toward religion that is too worldly in its concerns. It is the function of religion to console us as we experience our limitations, to reinforce faith, and to encourage discipline. In the latter respect, the alliance of the church and moderate forms of nationalism has found favor in conservative thought.

Conservatives view government with a mixture of respect and suspicion. Which of those attitudes a particular government evokes depends on two factors: how it is constituted and the role it plays with respect to other private and public institutions. Because conservatives have a rather low opinion of the average person's abilities, they are most suspicious of simple democracy. To unite a majority around a program the worth of which is allegedly proved by reason, without due regard for custom and tradition, is, from the conservative point of view, to invite the "tyranny of the majority." Conservatives see as particularly dangerous the kind of utopian democracy associated with the French Revolution, the Russian Revolution, and the utilitarian radicalism of Jeremy Bentham. A good government is constituted by good people: by the natural aristocracy of talent, breeding, and, very likely, wealth. An elite of experienced, disciplined, and moderate citizens is always to be preferred over a majority of the general population. Traditional conservatism is openly elitist.

If a government passes the test of proper construction, the traditional conservative insists on a second test: that it be limited in what it does and, within its sphere of action, that it be strong and resolute. The purpose of government is to maintain the framework of order within which other private institutions can operate effectively. Where the government oversteps its bounds is where it usurps the function of private institutions such as the family, the church, and the university.

Charity toward the poor is an obligation in any well-ordered society. That the poor should be looked after by the church, voluntary institutions, and personal philanthropy appeals to the traditional conservative as protection against the rise of collectivism and, ultimately, tyranny. The state should provide a minimal level of support to those who can't take care of themselves. However, if the government's social mission is too broadly defined, the conservative fears, a welfare mentality begins to degrade political relations. Democratic majorities will use governmental power to increase subsidies at the expense of the wealth of the truly productive people in the society.

In the conservative image of political life, the schools and universities have a special role. Liberals favor mass education and the "free marketplace of ideas"; conservatives quite explicitly endorse the notion that the purpose of an education is to instill the traditional wisdom of the society. Religion, as part of that tradition, is part of education. The curriculum should be an exercise in discipline for its own sake, as well as a conveyor of the cultural heritage.

Academic freedom is a relative concept for the conservative—and it is relative to what the conservative sees as the basic truths of the culture, which must not be denied by "false" teaching. Fundamental principles, rather than mere sensory experience, should be the subject of education. Otherwise, in the view of Richard Weaver, a traditionalist theorist, "With knowledge limited to sensory experience, man [is] eventually lost in 'endless induction' and 'multiplicities.' In sum, man "[has] been in retreat for centuries, from first principles, from definition, from true knowledge—that is, the knowledge of universals."[2] Religion and ethics should be taught in the schools; radical critiques of society should be downplayed or dispensed with.

The remainder of the institutions of the polity would be organized around voluntary interests. Traditionalists look with horror on unions that operate as internal democracies seeking the same treatment for all workers. Craft unions are regarded more favorably, since they are organized around conceptions of apprenticeship and seniority in the image of medieval guilds.

There seems to be a contradiction in the traditionalist view of political life. Conservatives believe in the dignity of the individual, on the one hand, and in order and hierarchy, on the other. But isn't the exercise of authority the principal threat to the dignity of the individual? Resolving this contradiction requires an understanding of the traditionalist view of human strengths and weaknesses. A noted conservative writer, Peter Viereck, once defined conservatism as "the political secularization of the doctrine of original sin."[3] The meaning of this is that institutions must do what the individual cannot do: provide the structures that will compensate for the limitations of human nature, while preserving the human potential for constructive action. People cannot fully develop without proper structures. The individual needs to be protected from weaknesses, nurtured in development, and given the means to express strengths.

The polity in these respects plays both a restraining role in relation to human weakness and a liberating role in cultivating individual potential. Robert Nisbet points out that "genuine freedom is not based upon the negative psychology of release. Its roots are in positive acts of dedication to ends and values. Freedom presupposes the autonomous existence of values that men wish to be free to follow and live up to. Such values are social in the precise sense that they arise out of, and are nurtured by, the voluntary associations which men form."[4] Paradoxically, freedom depends crucially on the role of institutions.

For all the emphasis on order in conservative thought, there is a key distinction between authority and power that separates legitimate from illegitimate order. Power, according to Nisbet, is simply the application of force without consent—as much a possibility in a majoritarian democracy as in a dictatorship. Authority, on the other hand, arises out of the "objectives and functions which command the response and talents" of people.[5] In Nisbet's view, authority is based on consent and commitment; power overrides consent and escapes limits. Conservatives attribute the rise of the powerful centralized state to the breakdown of legitimate authority. The key to the good society is that there should be a plurality of authorities serving many aspects of life. If the functions of these authoritative institutions overlap, that will serve the purpose of limiting and controlling the exercise of power.

■ Origins of Traditional Conservatism

An irony of the history of conservatism is that the use of the term *conservatism* to describe an ideology is actually rather recent. The term appeared in Europe in about 1830. Many strands constitute the roots of conservatism. To assemble this history is to pick out the leading themes, to reconstruct where they came from, and to see how they changed over time. It is in these origins and changes that the image of political life begins to take on various shades of meaning.

The history of conservatism is characterized by a series of unresolved arguments. These arguments reflect three basic tensions in conservative thought: the relative strength of *vice and virtue in human nature*, the *role of human action* in politics, and the appropriate *boundary between order and individual freedom*. As the preceding section suggests, the most important of these tensions involves estimating the weaknesses of human nature. It is the conservatives' view of human limitations that we have taken to be the hallmark of the conservative position.

The arguments over these tensions have changed because the modes of justification in Western culture have shifted: from natural law to theology, to rationalism (or, in this case, antirationalism), and on to historicism and nationalism. Each of these larger frameworks of thought offered conservatives a way of restating their central arguments. The fundamental problems of human vice, the role of personal action, and the nature of order have all received attention in natural-law philosophy, in theological defenses of monarchism, in conservative critiques of the revolutionary movements of the eighteenth and nineteenth centuries, and in conservative interpretations of the "meaning" of history and its implications for the destiny of nations. We will explore briefly the major developments arising from each of these modes of justification.

Conservatism and Natural Law

The oldest Western tradition of political theory comes from the natural-law philosophy of the Greeks and Romans. As we have seen, arguments based on natural law were used to set the basis for liberal individualism. However, there is another tendency in the natural-law tradition that helped to form conservative ideology.[6]

Natural-law philosophy places primary emphasis on the role of order in human life. Naturalism presupposes a meaning in life that lies behind appearances. For Plato and Aristotle, "reality" is not what we see around us; instead, reality is the inner principle that shapes these appearances. To understand these inner principles is to know the truth. Each human phenomenon thus contains the clues to some greater truth. So it is with political life. From the variety of political systems the Greeks observed, they attempted to distill the essence of politics.

The Greeks were not constrained by cultural assumptions of individualism: for them human beings are social creatures, or, in Aristotle's phrase, "Man is a political animal." Thus ideas about the good political life were the main subject of educated thought, and political philosophy was "the master science."

From this perspective, the polity is but human nature writ large—and it has the potential to reflect the virtues as well as the vices, strength as well as weakness. Because the potential for political life is both good and evil, the work of designing the *polis*, to use the Greek concept, is a matter of will and intention. Ernest Barker points out that "in saying that the state is natural, [Aristotle] does not mean that it 'grows' naturally, without human volition and action. . . . human agents 'construct' the state in co-operation with a natural immanent impulse."[7] So the work of creating the right form of polity is a matter for human action. It has to be conducted according to principles that can be discovered by the examination of human nature.

For traditional conservatives, political institutions have a dual role: they correct for human weakness and they express a natural order. Impelled by the urgency of liberating human virtue from the clutches of personal vice, the Greeks invite us to use observation and reason to understand the order that lies behind appearances and to fit our actions to it. Plato's own utopia, described in his *Republic*, is a blueprint for the assignment of individuals with particular qualities to appropriate positions in the polity. Whatever their other differences, Plato and Aristotle had a highly developed notion of the immanent order, and there was a large role for the most intelligent citizens to play. The culmination of this notion is Plato's philosopher-king, who is to apply the highest powers of the mind to the task of shaping the life of the polity.

Looking back on the Greek tradition, modern-day conservatives see too much rational design in Plato's *polis*. Modern conservatives do not associate themselves with the utopian style of the *Republic*. Conservatives are too skeptical for so large an act of faith. Yet traditionalists have never given up on the idea of a natural order. Given this view, the means of achieving the good polity is to select leaders who can shape institutions according to the proper conception of order. They prefer to put their trust in soundly constructed institutions rather than in schemes for achieving a perfect community.

Feudalism, Revolution, and the Rise of Conservatism

Conservatives have always wrestled with the problem of power. How can fallible human beings be entrusted with power sufficient to bring order to political life? Medieval theologians saw dangers in entrusting great power to the sovereign, but there was an infinitely greater danger in having no central power at all. Through their belief in original sin, these theologians could justify both the need for order and a reliance on divinely inspired monarchy. Only through divine inspiration of the ruler could God's requirement that there be order in human affairs be fulfilled without risking the abuses of tyranny. As this doctrine developed, feudalism, with its many protected statuses, gave way to absolute monarchy. The abuse of royal power led to the development of an opposition organized ultimately as a parliament.[8] The scene was set for the downfall of monarchical government.

What catalyzed the formation of conservative ideology was the century of the Enlightenment, the eighteenth century, culminating in the French Revolution of 1789. Prior to that time, the involvement of traditionalist ideas in the absolutist monarchies of Europe came under attack by both English liberals, with their radical notions of contractualism, and the French *philosophes*, whose rationalism and secularism undermined the basis of traditional politics.

With the French Revolution and all the excesses that followed, conservatives had their target and their opportunity. What conservatives such as Edmund Burke saw in the French Revolution was a perfect illustration of the beast in human nature, disguised in modernist clothing and turned loose to destroy society. It was precisely the elevation of *reason* over tradition, custom, habit, and settled practice that constituted the great evil of the Revolution. In Burke's eyes, secularism was the scaffold of the guillotine. Rationalism was the blade. By forsaking all the other institutions and customs through which human intelligence operates, society was made the victim of unbridled radicalism.

On the other hand, Burke approved of the American Revolution. He saw it as essentially an effort by the colonists to retrieve their traditional rights as Englishmen from the hands of a king who had abused customary rights. Here the villain is the monarch, and the heroes are the citizens. Burke was offering no blind endorsement of democracy, however, but rather an assertion that the people, at least the propertied class, could legitimately and forcefully protect their status from the threat of misguided authority. To locate the wisdom of the polity in its property holders rather than in the monarch, his or her ministers, or the aristocracy was an important initiative in conservative thought. It made of conservatism a contender in the new age of republican politics.

Burke was in fact more concerned with the method of change than with the agent. The political method he preferred was gradual, responsible, and carefully considered:

> The true lawgiver ought to have a heart full of sensibility. He ought to love and respect his kind, and to fear himself. It may be allowed to his temperament to catch his ultimate object with an intuitive glance, but his movements toward it ought to be deliberate. Political arrangement, as it is a work for social ends, is to be only wrought by social means . . . Time is required to produce that union of minds which alone can produce all the good we aim at.[9]

Burke thus attempted to liberate the traditionalist position from blind royalism, reduce its reliance on the mysteries of natural law, and make it a popular philosophy attractive to all thoughtful propertied citizens.

Conservatism, as N. K. O'Sullivan points out, is a "philosophy of imperfection, committed to the idea of limits, and directed towards the defense of a limited style of politics."[10] Conservatism as a political theory has survived in part because it has set this limited style of politics in opposition to the reformist, revolutionary, and totalitarian movements that have punctuated history since the time of the French Revolution. The subtitle of Peter Viereck's book *Conservatism Revisited: The Revolt Against Revolt* suggests the meaning of traditional conservatism for politics.

Modern Conservatism

We have seen how conservatism drew upon the natural-law tradition, relying on an abstract theory of a unified social order to justify a class-based hierarchy in political life. This basis for order fit with a conception of a world presided over by a single God and ministered to by an institutionalized church. Yet the association of religion with institutionalized power created, as Martin Luther pointed out, the possibility of manipulation by a privileged class of clergy who could use their power to dominate the polity.

It was the project principally of Georg Friedrich Hegel (1770–1831), along with such British thinkers as Samuel Taylor Coleridge (1772–1834) and Thomas Carlyle (1795–1881), to develop a framework that became a new rallying point for traditionalists seeking social unity. It was the theory that history has a meaning and that the nation-state is the carrier of that meaning. For these romantic conservatives, the national experience represented the release of a force that was propelling the achievement of ever "higher" levels of cultural expression. The task of politics was to find the inner logic of this plan and to facilitate its unfolding.

Nationalism: Historicism, Chauvinism, and the Rise of the "Mass Man"

Nationalism gave dynamism to conservative thought. The nation-state became the active agent of conservative designs. It expressed the moral order that traditionalists desired. Nationalism in Western European cultures represents a combination of forces, one lofty and philosophical and the other mundane and potentially murderous. These two forces are historicism and cultural chauvinism, and they are the different faces of the modern search for unity in Western society. The great difficulty of locating the meaning of history in the nation-state is that the nation is not simply a territory enclosed within boundaries; it is also racial and ethnic. The German conception of the Aryans as a master race destined to rule the world had its origins in the belief that the mystical collectivity of the German people, the *Volk*, had a meaning above and beyond individual life (see Chapter Nine).

The fascist horrors that followed upon the elaboration of *volkisch* ideology have obscured the traditionalist critique of fascism and of the more robust forms of nationalism. Isaiah Berlin, in summarizing the phenomenon of nationalism, identifies four characteristics of nationalism when it is in full flower: a sense of the *national group as distinct*, as expressive of an *organic unity in society*, as uniquely *ours as opposed to theirs*, and as *supreme* in the chauvinist sense.[11] Although various conservative writers and theorists have endorsed one or another of these attitudes toward the nation-state, traditionalist conservatism really only requires allegiance to one characteristic: the organicism of society—the conception that society is an interdependent whole with each person having an appropriate status and function. With respect to all other characteristics, the conservative commitment to a "limited style of politics," in O'Sullivan's phrase, precludes the belief in the nation-state in a chauvinist or xenophobic fashion.

A second political theme in contemporary conservatism grows

out of the fundamental concern for the requirements of an interdependent society. A favorite theme of conservative ideologues in the last fifty years has been the rise of what Jose Ortega y Gasset (1883–1955) labeled "the mass man."[12] For Ortega, the mass man is a person without judgment and principles. The mass man has only appetites. The capacity for creativity and for intelligent social relations is replaced by the illusion of self-sufficiency—and the reality of abdication to the power of the state.

In traditional conservative thought, the mass man was the conceptual opposite of the individual living in a properly constituted society. The distinction is subtler than one based merely on class. As Michael Oakeshott suggested, "the mass man is not necessarily 'ignorant,' often he is a member of the so-called intelligentsia; he belongs to a class which corresponds exactly with no other class." It is a class of people who claimed "the right to live in a social protectorate which relieved [them] from the burden of self-determination."[13] The mass man has no character. A nation-state of mass men would fall prey to tyranny.

A key difference between conservatives and liberals lies in what they mean by self-determination. For the traditional conservative, it means achieving the appropriate fit between personal character and the society's institutional requirements. The mass man is one who ignores the intricate code of institutionalized society as well as the burden of self-discipline, favoring instead the mindless assertion of appetite and a preference for publicly provided security. He is, in short, the conservative's caricature of the liberal individualist who follows a self-interested course of pursuing pleasure and avoiding pain.

Traditional conservatives think that if all individuals are left to pursue their own interests with a minimum of restraint, the result will be self-indulgence, anarchy, and a turn toward totalitarianism as the solution to the chaos that is created. Too much freedom in this simple, classically liberal sense will lead to the loss of freedom as defined in the subtler conception of the traditional conservative.

The Problem of the Marketplace

In the twentieth century, the traditional conservative's preference for hierarchy and institutionalism has been reflected in a critical attitude toward the role of the marketplace. The marketplace is seen as a democracy in the area of economics in which only dollars, not character or breeding, are counted. The problem the traditional conservatives have with the market stems from a concern for principles of justice. There are no precise principles of justice that are agreed upon, but there are images of the natural dignity of human beings and of a natural order arising out of the inherent differences among people. But what do these images mean for the marketplace? Edmund Burke endorsed the marketplace, though he "always assumed that Liberal capitalist economics could be kept subordinate to the Conservative social ethic."[14] Burke's preferred social ethic was based on the values of duty, honor, and chivalry. The conflict between money and principle was not resolved in Burke, nor is it in traditional conservatism generally.

In modern conservatism, there is a line of traditionalist thought that develops the position of "distributism."[15] The idea is that property should be widely distributed so as to maximize the number of people who have a stake in the preservation of an orderly society. Whereas radicals have favored this principle as a key to equality, some conservatives see it as a way of encouraging widespread affiliation with the organized institutional life of the community. Modern forms of this view include homesteading schemes and profit-sharing plans. Distributism is a means of extending the affiliation of citizens to the structures of elite power that comprise the vital institutions of the society.

■ Conclusion

The central problem of traditionalist conservatism has been to capture key political concepts in a formula that will provide a usable test of political action. The attraction of Bentham's liberal utilitarian formulation, "the greatest happiness of the greatest number," was its simplicity. Here was a test that could seemingly be applied to any policy question, with an answer provided by the simple mechanics of democracy. Conservatives have never solved that problem. The effort to ally traditionalism with nationalism has largely borne sour fruit. On the contemporary scene, distributism sounds too much like reform liberalism.[16] There remains no simple way to summarize what traditionalism means for contemporary life.

For all their difficulties, ideas that are labeled as conservative seem to have found a new appeal to electorates in industrialized countries. Their appeal is due partly to a reaction against the excesses of individual freedom that were perceived to have resulted from liberal policy initiatives. Social conservatism based on religious values is an historic theme in traditionalist thought. The difference now is that the pressure is coming from "fundamentalist" religions rather than from the more established institutions in the society.

More significant, however, is the creation of a conservative version of capitalism that relies on the marketplace as the paramount institution in society. The marketplace, the great creation of liberal individualism, has been appropriated by politicians calling themselves conservatives! How this new form of conservatism came into being, and what has become of the tension between justice and economic power in the marketplace, is the story of the next chapter on libertarian conservatism.

■ *Notes*

[1]Clinton Rossiter suggests that conservatism is more skepticism about change than an analysis of human nature: Clinton Rossiter, *Conservatism in America*, 2nd ed. rev. (New York: Random House, 1955), pp. 6–18. Yet Burke endorsed the American Revolution, and conservatives today advocate drastic changes in economic and social policy. Cf. Samuel Huntington's threefold classification of attitudinal differences among conservatives in "Conservatism as an Ideology," *American Political Science Review* (1958):454–473. More serviceable for our purposes is the division between traditional and libertarian conservatives found in George Nash, *The Conservative Intellectual Movement in the U.S. Since 1945* (New York: Basic Books, 1979), which is similar to the distinction between organic and individualist conservatism found in Kenneth and Patricia Dolbeare, *American Ideologies*, 3rd ed. (New York: Rand McNally, 1976).

[2]Summarized in George Nash, *The Conservative Intellectual Movement in the U.S. Since 1945* (New York: Basic Books, 1979), p. 40.

[3]Ibid., p. 66.

[4]Robert Nisbet, *The Quest for Community* (New York: Oxford University Press, 1962), p. 269.

[5]Ibid., p. xii.

[6]There is disagreement on whether natural law is an important basis for conservatism. Cf. Samuel Huntington, "Conservatism as an Ideology," *American Political Science Review* (1958) 454–473, and Russell Kirk, *The Conservative Mind: From Burke to Eliot*, 3rd ed. (Chicago: Regnery, 1960). Huntington associates conservatism with a defense of existing institutions rather than a commitment to the notion of an intrinsic order—an assumption central to natural law. Yet it is hard to see how a theory that depends on notions of order and prescription could escape a belief in a natural arrangement of human affairs.

[7]Aristotle, *The Politics*, Ernest Barker, trans. (New York: Oxford University Press, 1962), p. 7.

[8]For a fascinating study of feudal society, see Marc Bloch, *Feudal Society*, 2 vols. (Chicago: University of Chicago Press, 1961).

[9]Edmund Burke, *Reflections on the Revolution in France* (New York: Liberal Arts Press, 1790, 1955), p. 197.

[10]Noel O'Sullivan, *Conservatism* (New York: St. Martin's Press, 1976), p. 12.

[11]Isaiah Berlin, *Against the Current: Essays in the History of Ideas*, ed. by Henry Hardy (New York: Viking Press, 1980).

[12]Jose Ortega y Gasset, *The Revolt of the Masses*, anon. trans. (New York: Norton, 1932).

[13]Michael Oakeshott, "The Masses in Representative Democracy," in William Buckley, ed., *American Conservative Thought in the Twentieth Century* (New York: Bobbs-Merrill, 1970), pp. 118, 121.

[14]M. Morton Auerbach, *The Conservative Illusion* (New York: Columbia University Press, 1959), p. 37.

[15]Garry Wills, *Confessions of a Conservative* (New York: Penguin, 1979), pp. 135–142; cf. Auerbach, op. cit., pp. 106–130.

[16]See Daniel Patrick Moynihan's excellent study of what happened when a Republican administration tried to implement a form of guaranteed annual income as a replacement for welfare, in *The Politics of a Guaranteed Income: The Nixon Administration and the Family Assistance Plan* (New York: Random House, 1973).

FOUR

If one wishes to advocate a free society—that is, capitalism—one must realize that its indispensable foundation is
the principle of individual rights. If one wishes to uphold
individual rights, one must realize that capitalism is the
only system that can uphold and protect them.

Ayn Rand
The Virtue of Selfishness (1963)

Libertarian Conservatism and Anarchism

The conservative assumption that human beings are fallible and unequal can lead to a political conclusion other than the traditionalist prescription of institutionalized authority. That conclusion involves a total commitment to individual freedom. The argument is that individuals are so unique as to preclude any basis for a prescriptive order. There is no set of principles, such as superior experience or character, by which one individual can be given authority over another. Attempts to do so will usually result in fraud and corruption.

The minimization of government is the prime political objective. In the libertarian image of political life, the emphasis is on voluntary action; personal expression is supreme, and rarely is there to be found coercion, power, or force. The only function of government is the protection of people and property from physical harm inflicted by others.

In libertarianism, the free market is the essential institution and the metaphor for all other activities. Private enterprise is the vehicle for all economic activity and the model for public policy as well. Personal freedom is the central value, and inequality is accepted as the natural result of free behavior.

On the left, the libertarian movement meets with the anarchist tradition. Anarchists assume that, once governmental institutions are no longer there to inhibit and repress our sense of humanity, there will be a great profusion of community activity. People will engage in all kinds of selfless mutuality and cooperation. Thus anarchists see the overthrow of state authority as opening the door to the good side of human nature. Libertarians, on the other hand, are more likely to see the removal of governmental power as a realistic accommodation to self-interested human nature. Fundamentally what separates libertarianism from anarchism is the conservative's pessimistic assumption about the limitations of human nature.

Although libertarians and anarchists share some basic ideas and cite some of the same sources, their respective views of human nature are quite distinctive. These contrasting versions of life in a society with sharply limited government bring into focus the uses and abuses of governmental power in political ideologies. By looking at them side by side, it is possible to see more clearly the implicit assumptions each has about human nature and the meaning of politics. After exploring the libertarian image of political life, its sources, and its implications for the conservative movement, we will contrast libertarian conservatism with anarchism.

■ *The Libertarian Image of Political Life*

In the ideal community of the libertarian, there is little taxation, minimal welfare, and no conscription. No creed of any kind, religious or otherwise, is enforced. Private property is virtually inviolate.

Nearly all restrictions on private enterprise should be eliminated, save a minimum of regulations designed to protect the environment. Regulation itself should operate through the marketplace. The manufacturer, and ultimately the consumer, should bear the full costs of a production process. Damage done by stripmining, for example, should be paid for by the producer and reclaimed through the cost of coal, rather than by taxation for environmental clean-up.

The ability of the government to use its political power would be severely restricted. Public services would be placed on a user-payment basis. To the greatest extent possible, political organization would devolve to the neighborhood level.

Limited government avoids an evil identified in the conservative suspicion of human fallibility. The power of officials can't be as easily abused when it is so carefully circumscribed. Taxation and regulation are conceived of as the means for the entrenchment of advantage and position. All activity that is structured around collective consent or majority rule contains the danger that the weak will, through numbers, overtake and victimize the strong and the creative. The market, on the other hand, rewards the latter group, and they are society's most useful people.

For libertarians, the suspicion of power extends as much to big business as it does to big government. Government is the means by which big business can gain a position that pure competition in the marketplace would never allow. The libertarians find in almost all governmental undertakings the effort to use the force of government to obtain what should be had with legitimacy only through the free market, whether of goods or ideas.

The effort to provide a common basic education for all citizens has, in the libertarian view, led to mediocrity and conformity. The use of legal force to keep unwilling students in school has undermined the learning experience. The libertarian conservative would introduce competition into elementary and secondary school systems. Rather than having a single public school system, libertarians would prefer that students be given vouchers that could be used to finance an education at the school of their choice. Forcing competition among schools would result in higher quality.

Restrictions on personal behavior are also removed. Laws against drug abuse are to be repealed and individuals held responsible for their own behavior. Sexual behavior is likewise regulated only by personal responsibility for the consequences. Society has little or no mission to perform in salvaging people from their mistakes. A full burden of responsibility is placed on every person.

For the libertarian, as for the classical liberal, such political community as there may be depends on individual initiative. The estimate as to how much civic activity there will be varies in the libertarian movement. Some libertarians have worked with neighborhood self-sufficiency movements to see if voluntary activity could become well developed enough to take care of many community functions.[1] On the far right of the movement is Ayn Rand's utopia, to be found in her novel *Atlas Shrugged*, where every interindividual transaction is reduced to selfish calculations of mutual utility and personal favors are repaid in cash.[2]

■ *History of Libertarian Conservatism*

The history of libertarian conservatism is simple to tell, apart from a certain confusion about the labels used to describe it. The problem with the labels is that its sponsors often call themselves conservatives, while acknowledging that libertarianism has its primary roots in classical liberalism.

There are two reasons for this anomaly. Libertarianism is an ultraindividualist theory. In that sense, it claims to represent something special about the Western tradition prior to the rapid growth of state power in the 1930s. Thus, individualist libertarians see themselves as *conservators* of an earlier political and economic tradition—even if that tradition may more properly be labeled classical liberalism.

Libertarians also identify with much of conservatism's traditional analysis of human nature. Libertarians believe that, imperfect as people may be, the best hope for the humane life lies in individual freedom. They concede less to the power of rationality than classical liberals do and appreciate much more the idiosyncratic and unique character of individual life. The libertarian individualist is, in short, something of a heroic figure battling against mass mediocrity, a romantic conservative's answer to the utility calculating economic man of the Benthamites. It is in these overtones of struggle, best evidenced in the work of Ayn Rand, that one can see the pessimism of the conservative showing through.

The roots of libertarianism are found in the writings of Adam Smith and the group of late eighteenth- and early nineteenth-century writers, largely businessmen, known as the Manchester School of English utilitarians. What Smith promoted as laissez faire for reasons of economic efficiency and moral discipline, the Manchester School advertised as the key to individual freedom for its own sake. In the hands of Herbert Spencer (1820–1903), the doctrine was restated as Social Darwinism. The market was the means of natural selection among human beings. The "fittest" would survive its rigorous tests and would succeed. The weak would fail—but that is nature's and, according to Spencer, society's way. Setting aside the phenomenon of cooperation in nature, and the differences that human intelligence and social sensitivity might make among human beings, Spencer proclaimed competition as the natural principle of human life.

Antistatism

It remained for two Austrian economists, Friedrich Hayek and his student Ludwig Von Mises, writing in the spirit of crisis of the 1930s and 1940s, to identify the original Manchester tradition and free enterprise capitalism as the mainsprings of Western culture.[3] Some scholars saw the advent of totalitarianism in Germany as the reaction to excessive individualism, competition, and the rise of industrial capitalism. Hayek and Von Mises saw it rather as the consequence of the advance of "statism" and of the notion that the state could provide security for the individual. The resulting breakdown of individual self-reliance made the Germans ripe for tyranny.[4]

The state and even the concept of security itself were seen as the enemies. Only the uncompromising assertion of individual self-determination could protect us from the conniving of craven security-seekers who would undermine our liberties and even deliver us up to totalitarianism.[5] This was the theme of early libertarian manifestos and has remained as the consistent, though somewhat moderated, refrain ever since.

Libertarians shared the traditional conservative's disdain for the "mass man." It is typical of the difference between them, however, that the libertarians prescribed a quite different solution from the reinstitution of appropriate forms of authority. For them the threat was not in the personal weaknesses of the mass man but in the governmental institutions that removed the need for self-reliance. Were men truly free, they would lose their massness and become genuinely responsible.[6]

This moral tone in libertarian thought derives from a basic commitment libertarians share—a commitment that separates libertarians from traditional conservatives. Morality consists in the exercise of individual choice. Behavior that is not freely chosen has no moral standing in libertarian eyes. It is the making of personal judgments that "leads some people to moral excellence and others to moral failure."[7]

The state is deeply suspect in libertarian thought. Murray Rothbard formulates the attitude toward the state in stark and simple terms:

> If, then, the State is not "us," if it is not "the human family" getting together to decide mutual problems, if it is not a lodge meeting or country club, what is it? Briefly, the State is that organization in society which attempts to maintain a monopoly of the use of force and violence in a given territorial area; in particular, it is the only organization in society that obtains its revenue not by voluntary contribution or payment for services rendered, but by coercion.[8]

By a "monopoly of the use of force" Rothbard is referring to the policing functions that give law its means of enforcement.

Thus the state is the enemy of choice and therefore of individuality. The case against the state acquires a moral dimension: it is evil because it is precisely the agency that denies choice to those who oppose its decisions. Since choice is the beginning point of all morality, government and the coercion that is its method of operation are morally suspect.

In terms of the development of libertarian thought, the events of the late 1960s and early 1970s turned out to be quite consequential. Many libertarians separated themselves from the conservative establishment over the issue of the Vietnam War, and especially the draft, and went on to build a substantially separate movement. The movement centered on resistance to the statism that libertarians see as pervasive in the rest of American society.[9]

Karl Hess, a former speech writer for conservative Republican Presidential candidate Barry Goldwater, became an exponent of libertarianism as an alternative to the "system" politics of the conventional conservative movement. Hess became involved in an ambitious effort to establish a workable alternative community oriented to "understandable work, friends, someplace to stand, a reason to stand up, and a certainty of being counted, of being heard, of being a recognizable and not an indistinguishable part of the whole."[10] Freed of statist coercion, personal uniqueness could be restored. The numbing conformity of an institutionalized society could be overthrown.

The effort toward decentralizing and simplifying technology in order to meet human needs at the neighborhood and community level is a vital part of this movement. Technology is explicitly addressed as a key to self-sufficiency. Although the initial experiment in the Adams-Morgan neighborhood of Washington, D.C., did not survive after five years of innovative experimentation in neighborhood self-sufficiency, the rhetoric of the movement found its way into the Reagan administration's emphasis on neighborhood-based self-help strategies for fighting urban blight and central city deterioration.

The libertarian movement represents the fulfillment of the anti-community bias of classical liberal thought, with an added motif of suspicion and even hostility regarding all things governmental. What remains is a contradiction within the contemporary conservative movement. The traditional conservative and the libertarian are thus sharply split over the meaning and uses of authority.

■ The Traditionalist–Libertarian Split

In comparing the two tendencies of conservative thought, George Nash points out that "While libertarians stressed the freedom of the individual in opposition to the State, traditionalists saw in the 'masterless man' a threat. While libertarians asserted the *right* of the individual to be free, the *right* to be oneself, traditionalists were concerned with what an individual *ought* to be."[11] In this contrast lies the difference between the two conservatisms. The libertarians are, for nearly all purposes, hostile to the notion of political community; the traditionalists regard community institutions as the primary vehicles of their philosophy.

The implications for community are clear. For libertarians, it is the capacity for choice that separates human beings from lower animals, and it is therefore the mission of the community to provide the circumstances in which free choice can be exercised most fully. Morality consists in minimizing structure and maximizing individual freedom. Traditional conservatives see the matter quite differently. Judgment is also important to a traditional conservative, but continuity and custom are more significant than independence and choice. Morality consists in judgment exercised within the confines of these sobering influences. Again, for traditionalists, the role of the community is precisely to nourish those structures that will constrain choice within appropriate boundaries.

Just as traditional conservatives are reluctant to make unrestricted individual choice the centerpiece of their philosophy, so are they unwilling to see the state as the enemy of morality. For example, the use of state power to prohibit abortions, to mandate the offering of prayer in public schools, to enforce capital punishment, and, above all, to strengthen police power (whether locally or internationally through the military) are issues that separate libertarians from traditional conservatives. Libertarians generally oppose these measures; traditional conservatives support them.

It is here that traditionalists, their banner taken up by religious fundamentalists, meet libertarians in open confrontation. It is the traditional conservative appreciation of legitimate authority that has become the wellspring of the revolt against "permissiveness," with its consequences for such issues as the family, censorship, prayer in the schools, and sexual equality. The chosen instrument of this revolt is governmental action—whether to build up the military, enforce school prayer, forbid abortion, or censor library books.

The conflict within the conservative movement between traditionalists and libertarians is ultimately deeper than even these sharp programmatic differences suggest. Libertarianism is a democratic form of conservatism. All individuals are given the same freedoms from restraint by the state and other institutions. Traditionalism, by contrast, is not classless. It is precisely differentiations in authority, based in class differences, that provide the means of social control within the context of powerful institutions.

The split finally comes home at the community level. If all social and political functions are subsumed in the service of the marketplace, the results for community may be quite the opposite of the traditionalist design. The continuity of community institutions, the stability of the family, the authority of the church, the independence of universities, and the fabric of social mores may all be dissolved by the acid of self-interest. Ultimately, in such social aggregations as these, there may be little of the institutional pluralism that distinguishes traditional conservatism and little of the democracy that distinguishes libertarianism. Power may drift into the hands of the best organized and the advantaged, with the rest left to shift for themselves.

Alternatively, as political power declines, economic power increases in significance. In our system, political power has seemingly become more democratic, while economic power arguably has become more concentrated. Libertarians may discover that the consequence of freeing the market from relatively democratic political control will be an increase in the economic power and political preeminence of a traditionalist upper class—a class that has historically favored stronger limits on personal behavior and more substantial forms of institutional control.

What holds these two conservatisms together in the current political scene is, very probably, the fact that by pursuing the libertarian program of reducing taxation, no one benefits so much as the traditional upper class. Whether that class will remain content with the results for social order of the decline in the role and strength of governmental institutions is one of the key questions for the future of the movement.

■ An Anarchist Perspective

Much less visible on the nightly news than conservatism is an ideology that has had a powerful influence on Western political history as well as American radicalism: anarchism. The term derives from the Greek roots *an-archy*, meaning literally "without a leader." Anarchists, along with libertarians, believe that the legitimation of the use of force through the state is the problem in society, not the solution, as in most other ideologies. However, anarchists are sensitive to sources of coercion apart from the state. The concentration of economic power through the institution of unlimited private property concerns them greatly. They are also suspicious of technology. Anarchists see in technology a tendency toward increasing the amount of hierarchy and domination in society. We will explore each of these themes briefly.

"Property is theft!" Pierre Proudhon (1809–1865) made this the rallying cry of anarchists determined to undo the basis of capitalism. His argument in a famous pamphlet, *What Is Property?* (1840), was that nature belongs to all humankind and that the use of it should be shared by groups of people living and working together in voluntary cooperation. The notion of appropriating a piece of nature, calling it "mine," and erecting a government to coerce people into respecting its ownership is the root of the class system and the wholesale abuse of power that goes with it.

This argument finds modern reflection in the work of Murray Bookchin. In his *The Ecology of Freedom: The Emergence and Dissolution of Hierarchy*, he argues that the principle of *usufruct* should replace that of private property. In capitalism, private property can be acquired and kept almost irrespective of what is done with it; Bookchin makes an anarchist argument for the principle of usufruct: "resources should belong to the user as long as they are being used." In a truly free society, the use made of resources would express both a communal and an individual need. "A collective need subtly orchestrates work, not personal need alone. . . . Hence, even the work performed in one's own dwelling has an underlying collective dimension in the potential availability of its products to the entire community."[12] He foresees a kind of spontaneous socialism that would operate by consent based on mutual need.

At root, anarchists believe that common sense will make evident the shared nature of basic needs once all the distortions introduced by institutionalized power are removed. The specialized, class-ridden system of production and distribution we now have must be dismantled. When work is specialized and regimented, it becomes alienating. All traces of individual creativity are removed. Management substitutes for initiative, private coercion for personal incentive. In capitalism, the race for survival permits exploitation of workers by managers, managers by stockholders, and stockholders by financial speculators. Everyone is set against everyone else.

True liberty will allow human beings to develop fully as the social creatures they are capable of becoming. Society will become the positive expression of human nature rather than the oppressive instrument of dominant classes.[13] Anarchists rely heavily on accounts of primitive or isolated societies, such as that of the Eskimos, to make their point.[14] Whereas anarchists realize that absolute equality would itself require the forceful suppression of differences, they argue that all human beings have similar basic needs. In a just society, those minimal needs could be met through common action. What goes beyond the minimum is for each individual to work out either alone or with others.

The principle of voluntarism, which is at the heart of anarchism, shapes the conception of politics found in anarchist writings. Anarchists distrust representative democracy as an invitation to the tyranny of the majority. It is, in the words of one anarchist theoretician, a "grand lottery" with no guarantee that the result will be characterized by wisdom or virtue. Anarchists prefer direct, as opposed to representative, democracy. Society needs to be broken down into groups that are capable of face-to-face exchange and common decision making. Participatory democracy is contrasted with representative democracy operating through politicians. Democracy without direct personal participation becomes a means of avoiding responsibility and opens the door to manipulation and corruption.

Technology and Hierarchy

Anarchists extend their rebellion against domination to the realm of technology. Modern anarchists do not reject technology per se, but they do see it as a dangerous phenomenon that must be used

carefully on a scale permitting individual control and the maintenance of humane values.[15] Most recently, anarchists have attempted to incorporate their concern with technology into an
ecological framework, arguing that the unity of our natural existence must be restored if we are not to destroy the planet. It is the
capacity of technology to separate us from the natural environment that is its greatest danger. The renewal of constructive and
nurturing modes of exchange with nature are advanced as the cure
for this malady.[16]

As a political movement, anarchism has influenced terrorists as
well as pacifists.[17] In the decades prior to the First World War, six
heads of state were assassinated by terrorists, including an American President, William McKinley. The anarchists were a major
force in the Spanish Civil War (1936–1939), and their retribution
against those who held power, whether through politics, property,
or the church, was direct and brutal.[18] More recently, anarchist
thought deeply influenced the countercultural left in the antiwar
era of the sixties and early seventies as radicals attempted to
broaden the movement into a generalized revolt against "the system" and all the relations of domination found in politics, education, culture, and personal life.

For all that can be said about anarchist conceptions of how
society might work, it remains, as one commentator put it, "less a
political philosophy than it is a temperament. . . . Anarchism
means . . . a grand struggle against evil, a secular crusade against
the debasement of self, a fight against social degradation that the
idea and the reality of the state seem to represent."[19] It is this
temperament that influences anarchist modes of artistic and
cultural criticism, as well as political agitation.

■ *Conclusion*

By examining libertarianism and anarchism together, we can see
how government is but one relationship of authority in our lives.
There are many others. Anarchists try to account for the whole
structure of domination. Contemporary libertarians are mainly
concerned with only one source of domination: government. From
an anarchist point of view, the reduction of governmental authority without the commensurate reduction of economic (and
religious, and social) authority would simply mean that those
sources of coercive power would grow in significance with no
necessary gain in true liberty.

A quite different perspective on the uses of power is provided by the next chapter on reform liberalism. Here we will see power of one kind—political power—used to counterbalance and regulate power of other kinds: economic and social.

■ *Notes*

[1]David Morris and Karl Hess, *Neighborhood Power: The New Localism* (Boston: Beacon Press, 1975). Morris and Hess draw on a combination of anarchist and libertarian themes in attempting to revive the neighborhood as a meaningful center of political life.

[2]Cf. Jerome Tucille, *It Usually Begins with Ayn Rand: A Libertarian Odyssey* (New York: Stein and Day, 1972).

[3]Kenneth Dolbeare and Patricia Dolbeare, *American Ideologies: The Competing Political Beliefs of the 1970s*, 3rd ed. (Chicago: Rand McNally, 1976), pp. 60–62.

[4]Friedrich Hayek, *The Road to Serfdom* (Chicago: University of Chicago Press, 1944).

[5]This generalization provides the libertarian theme in William F. Buckley's blend of libertarianism and traditional conservatism. William F. Buckley, *Up from Liberalism* (New York: Honor Books, 1959).

[6]Ayn Rand, *Capitalism: The Unknown Ideal* (New York: Signet Books, 1966).

[7]Tibor Machan, ed., *The Libertarian Alternative* (Chicago: Nelson Hall, 1974), p. 499.

[8]Ibid., p. 70. Rothbard's antistatist arguments provide a text for both libertarians and anarchists. See Alan Ritter, *Anarchism: A Theoretical Analysis* (Cambridge: Cambridge University Press, 1981), p. 180.

[9]Jerome Tucille, *Radical Libertarianism* (Indianapolis, Ind.: Bobbs-Merrill, 1970). Cf. Irving Kristol, *On the Democratic Ideal in American Life* (New York: Harper & Row, 1972), and Kristol's critique of libertarianism in *Two Cheers for Capitalism* (New York: Basic Books, 1978).

[10]Karl Hess, *Community Technology* (New York: Harper & Row, 1979), p. 4.

[11]George Nash, *The Conservative Intellectual Movement in the U.S. Since 1945* (New York: Basic Books, 1979), p. 82.

[12]Bookchin, *The Ecology of Freedom* (Palo Alto, Calif.: Chesire Books, 1982) p. 50.

[13]For the early history of these sentiments in the United States, see Staughton Lynd, *The Intellectual Origins of American Radicalism* (Cambridge, Mass.: Harvard University Press, 1982), p. 110.

[14]Bookchin, op. cit., p. 51.

[15]See E. F. Schumacher, *Small Is Beautiful: Economics as if People Mattered* (New York: Harper & Row, 1976).

[16]See Bookchin, op. cit., p. 315 ff. Cf. Mulford Q. Sibley, *Nature and Civilization: Some Implications for Politics* (Notre Dame University Press, 1981).

[17]On the latter, see William O. Reichert, *Partisans of Freedom: A Study of American Anarchism* (Bowling Green, Ohio: Bowling Green University Press, 1976).

[18]Murray Bookchin, *Spanish Anarchists, Heroic Years 1868–1936* (New York: Harper & Row, 1978).

[19]Terry Perlin, *Contemporary Anarchism* (San Francisco, Calif.: Transaction Books, 1979), p. 3.

FIVE

The first duty of the government is to the weak.

Lorenzo Dow Lewelling,
Populist Governor of Kansas,
in the "Tramp Circular" (1893)

Reform
Liberalism

Reform liberalism brings together ideas taken from populism, progressivism, and even socialism. These ideas came together in the New Deal, President Franklin Delano Roosevelt's response to the near collapse of the economy in the early 1930s. It is a movement that has gone through many phases over the past fifty years and reached a peak in the "Great Society" programs of President Lyndon Johnson (1963–1969). Since then, the reform liberal agenda has declined in influence under sustained assault by conservatives led most effectively by President Ronald Reagan.

Reform liberalism may more properly be the name of a movement than of an ideology, yet there is a thread that ties reform liberalism together and distinguishes it from other ideologies.[1] That limited vision is simply the notion that government should act to assist disadvantaged individuals so that they can compete effectively in the marketplace. Reform liberalism was not conceived by one systematic thinker. What began as an amalgam of ideas from many sources was trimmed and shaped by the practicalities of politics, leaving in place only those parts of the New Deal that conformed with a limited vision of reform.

Reform liberals do not set out to abolish the marketplace, but rather to use governmental power to remedy the inequalities of opportunity that it produces. It is still liberalism because it conceives of equality in terms of *opportunity* rather than *end result*. Reform liberalism also maintains the liberal focus on individual self-interest as the heart of politics. But the central objective is to use government to see that all citizens have a reasonable chance of participating in a competitive society.

Classical liberals and reform liberals can be differentiated by understanding the distinction between *negative* and *positive* liberty. Negative liberty means a lack of obstacles to free choice. Classical liberalism provided negative liberty by authorizing a system of private property and individual rights that protected the possessions of one person from invasion by another. The free choice of what to do with one's possessions was not to be limited by the obstacles of theft and violence. Similarly, classical liberalism restricted the power of government to interfere with freedom of expression and other basic rights.

Reform liberals accept this program, but they wish to go further. Even with every obstacle removed, some people may not have the positive means of exercising free choice. The unavailability of jobs, educational deficiencies, illness, the effects of racism, and poverty itself can mean that individuals find their options severely limited. The lack of obstacles doesn't necessarily bring with it the realistic possibility of having choices in life. Reform liberals attempt to remedy this imbalance through the concept of positive liberty. Positive liberty refers to having the substantive means of overcoming deficiencies so that genuine options are available; for example, education, health care, and job programs. The instrument of reform liberalism is governmental assistance.

Since governmental action is essential to this vision, the processes of government are themselves the target of reformist politics. The movement assumed that politics could be made honest through democratic reforms that would allow the plurality of interests in the United States to be fairly represented. A reformed process of government was to be the key to a reformed society.

We will see how this ideological vision plays itself out in the reformist image of the good society. With this image in mind, we will turn our analysis to understanding the ideas that were borrowed from progressivism and populism to change the agenda of American politics and shape new policies through several administrations beginning with the New Deal.

■ The Reformist Vision of the Good Society

Classical liberalism has one great flaw: to celebrate individualism is to accept extremes of economic inequality that leave some people far ahead of others in even the most basic prerequisites for a decent life. Historically, liberalism was a radical doctrine aimed at freeing individuals from the stifling hand of a hierarchical feudal society to pursue their own interests freely. The old order of separate "estates" and obligations for different classes was overthrown. Through the institution of private property, classical liberals transformed the communitarian basis of feudalism and created a society based on individual self-interest and contract. The consequence was a dynamic and individualistic society, but one in which vast inequalities separate the advantaged and the strong from the disadvantaged and the weak.

At the beginning of this chapter, reform liberalism was defined as a movement centered on using government to assist individuals so that they might have the substantive means of competing in a market society. What would it take to provide everyone with a chance of competing on a reasonable basis? The most obvious answers have to do with health, education, and economic welfare. Each of these deals with substantive personal problems and misfortunes that can disable and handicap.

In the reformist vision of society, health care would be insured privately when possible and publicly when necessary. No one would be without medical care for serious illnesses and injuries. In addition, government would actively pursue disease control, the regulation of industry to avoid health hazards, and the administration of fair standards and pricing in health care institutions.

Similarly, education would be a public responsibility. Reform liberals share the classical liberals' commitment to rationality as the method of a civilized society. Consequently, good public education is an objective that involves the very foundation of the society. What reformers added to the program was the active encouragement of those previously excluded from the educational system by either lack of money, discrimination, or deficiency of background.

From preschool programs through graduate education, those whose performance is limited by family background, income, deficiencies in basic skills, racial and ethnic barriers, and malnutrition would, through national, state, or local government programs, be offered extra classes, special tutoring, and personal support in the form of guidance and even income and subsidized meals. Educational institutions would be required to give preference to the hiring of teachers from disadvantaged groups. Admissions quotas would be established to ensure that disadvantaged groups have access to scarce places in professional schools. The educational process is the central channel for improving the upward mobility of the disadvantaged.

No one is to be denied the chance of living at a minimal standard of decency. Minimum income maintenance would be the right of all citizens. For those who are temporarily unemployed, there are government-guaranteed unemployment benefits. Government programs supply unemployment counseling, retraining, and employment services. Publicly financed work is available to those unable to find employment. Projects such as building and maintaining public facilities and staffing public services would provide jobs. Private employers are subsidized by the government for hiring the unemployed.

The lack of motivation that afflicts some of the poor would be dealt with by professionals trained in counseling, guiding, motivating, and organizing the disadvantaged. Rather than simply redistributing income directly, most reform liberals have advocated the extensive use of social services. The services should be coordinated so that a person unemployed because of ill health would be provided with medical assistance, family counseling, food stamps, employment training, and job placement services. The linking of these services would afford a coordinated approach to individual assistance.

Access to competition is opened up by strict enforcement of antitrust and price-fixing laws. Regulations to encourage bidding by minority firms bring in those previously excluded from the marketplace. Reforms of employment examinations to remove quotas on hiring, racial biases and unnecessary requirements, and the enforcement of antidiscrimination laws are designed to open employment opportunities to all.

Racism, which handicaps minorities in the competitive struggle, is to be vigorously opposed by governmental action. Segregation of public accommodations such as hotels and restaurants is made illegal. Discrimination, whether in hiring, admissions to educational institutions, or public transportation, is outlawed. Public policy is redirected to give first consideration to previously excluded minorities in all aspects of hiring and promotion.

The denial of political rights through restrictions on voter registration or access to the polls is corrected by action of the federal government against offending local officials. To ensure the integrity and openness of the political process, reform liberals would use laws to regulate the nomination of candidates for public office. Primary elections or nominating caucuses open to all those willing to declare a party preference increase the effectiveness of democracy at the grass-roots level. The old system of nomination by power-brokers and party "bosses" is cast aside in favor of these new procedures.

Civil liberties are protected from violation by government, private organizations, and even private individuals. The original conception of the Bill of Rights of the U.S. Constitution was that individuals must be protected from governmental interference in their freedom of expression. But what about threats to freedom of expression from private groups such as the Ku Klux Klan, or a self-appointed censor, or an employer? Reform liberals would make the enforcement of civil liberties protections an active responsibility of government through legislation, executive leadership, and legal challenges in the courts.

The fundamental assumption of reform liberalism is that governmental action can overcome inequalities in background, wealth, and most especially power. Making the political process fair and open to all is a primary objective. Since political campaigns depend on expensive media advertising, campaign finance regulation goes to the core of the political process. Reform liberals want to be sure that elections cannot be bought by special interests or wealthy contributors. Limitations on private contributions, public reporting requirements, and the availability of public funding are used to prevent the buying of elections by special interests and wealthy contributors. These measures are intended to compensate for the political disadvantages of the poor and unorganized and assure open access to the political process.

In the workplace, as in politics, reform liberals want to make the arrangement of power fairer. The right of people to organize unions for the purposes of bargaining with their employers over wages and working conditions is protected by law. This option provides a basic tool for those who do not own the means of production to develop the power to confront those who do. The process of collective bargaining would be regulated to define unfair practices, establish grievance procedures, and ensure honest elections of union officers.

Reform liberals stop short of endorsing measures aimed at absolute equality, such as drastic income redistribution. They do, however, believe that government can be an active and effective agent on behalf of the disadvantaged.[2] What we have seen is a sketch of the reform liberal's ideal society. Other illustrations of the extension of reform liberalism to environmental policy, attitudes toward foreign policy, and the protection of minorities will appear as we discuss the emergence of these ideas and the movement that carried them forward.

■ The History of Reform Liberalism

The origins of American reform liberalism really go back to the beginnings of the country. There was from the earliest period of European settlement a tradition of thought that diverged from the notion of individual self-interest as a basis for the "social contract." Whatever John Locke may have said about the influence of appetites and interests in shaping behavior and necessitating a social contract to provide order (see Chapter Two), there is also in Locke a claim that people have a certain natural reasoning ability, and with that certain rights. The authors of the Declaration of Independence incorporated Locke's notion of government by consent in the context of a claim for equality and natural rights based on God's will (emphasis mine):

> We hold these truths to be self-evident, that all men are created equal, *that they are endowed by their Creator with certain unalienable Rights, that among these are Life, Liberty, and the pursuit of Happiness.* That to secure these rights,

Governments are instituted among Men, deriving their just powers from the consent of the governed. That whenever any Form of Government becomes destructive of these ends, it is the Right of the People to alter or to abolish it, and to institute new Government, laying its foundation on such principles and organizing its powers in such form, *as to them shall seem most likely to effect their Safety and Happiness.*

If human beings are created equal, and if government is to serve the rights of all, then government must be something more than the policeman for the property owners.[3] The Declaration argues that rights come not from the ownership of property but from God or, in a more secular version, from an "equal creation." Benjamin Franklin, Thomas Jefferson, Thomas Paine, and numerous others struggled over the relationship between property, individual rights, and the rights of the community as a whole. All endorsed the notion of private property, but they saw it as the creation of the community and as beholden to it in some limited sense.[4] Jefferson and Paine, in particular, distinguished the ownership of property as a civil right, accorded by society, from permanent and inalienable natural rights attached to human existence. That distinction became the basis for efforts to regulate inheritance and for proposals, rarely successful, to allow for government redistribution of land.[5]

Throughout American history there have been profound struggles over the issue of property versus human rights. The notion that slaves are people rather than property was a basic factor in the U.S. Civil War. Efforts by debtors to weaken the power of creditors through monetary reform and efforts to limit the powers of banks are frequent occurrences in our political history.[6] What we will explore here is the contribution of the best-known movements to the creation of a reform liberal tradition that came of age in the New Deal program of Franklin Roosevelt.[7] These movements include *populism, socialism,* and *progressivism.* Socialism will be dealt with in Chapter Seven; however, populism and progressivism are crucial to the background of the New Deal as well as to the continuing struggle over the meaning of equality for the process and policies of American government.

Populism

Populism has the same root word as "people." Populist movements claim to speak for the "little people" against the big interests. Historically, populists were concerned with two related kinds of inequality: wealth and power. The revolt against concentrations of wealth are the better-known part of the populist program, though recently the term "populist" has been revived by libertarian conservatives who want to reduce the power exercised by government in the marketplace.

As John Diggins notes in his history of the American Left, the populist People's Party in the 1890s "could control or influence a dozen state legislatures and claim four senators and over fifty congressmen."[8] The movement, consisting of various parties and factions, was based in the pressures felt by small farmers beset by debt, railroad monopolies, and land speculators. To confront these forces, populists advocated government credit, railroad regulation, antitrust laws, and election reforms. The idea is to counterbalance the power of the wealthy minority with the power of the activated majority.

For all that populists sought to achieve by governmental action, however, they were not socialists. The socialists' distaste for private property ran against the grain of a movement that was part of the American experience of small landholdings and personal advancement through hard work. Populists believed in active government on behalf of the average citizen, not the replacement of capitalism by a planned economy.[9]

Originating largely among farmers in the South and Midwest, populism carried with it certain prejudices as well as a political program, though the two were tied together.[10] In the South, many populists were also racists who saw the suppression of blacks as a key to maintaining the precarious position of poor white dirt farmers. Efforts to ally poor blacks and whites under the populist banner ended in failure. In other areas, populists were anti-Catholic and saw the big-city Catholic political machines as corrupt and powerful enemies. Whether populists were any more nativist and chauvinist than the general population is open to dispute; however, the populist feeling of being victimized by other groups politicized prejudices in a powerful fashion. Anti-Semitism, expressed as resentment against Jewish financiers and media interests, is still a part of populist movements in parts of the South and Midwest.

The People's Party declined rapidly after 1896, largely because much of its program was taken over by Democrats and progressive Republicans. As one historian remarked,

[Populism's] demands anticipated many changes to come in the twentieth century. If the demands for the recovery of public lands were never met, they anticipated the rationale of the conservation movement, the land as a public heritage. If the railroads were never nationalized, they experienced more effective state and federal regulation. And if the populists never elaborated a program for controlling the trusts, their condemnation of abuses in business helped advance corporate regulation and antitrust measures. Their demands for changes in political and electoral practices read almost like a catalog of twentieth-century reforms in that field.[11]

In the 1980s the label *populist* has been claimed by both Left and Right. Conservative populists, angry over the actions of the Supreme Court in outlawing school prayer and protecting the civil rights of suspected criminals, have mounted a campaign to reverse these decisions through a constitutional convention.[12] Part of a broader reaction against permissiveness in American culture, the leaders of this movement have termed it "populist" because they see themselves rebelling against policies made by governmental elites. These elites, they say, are out of touch with popular feeling.[13]

Populists of the Left in contemporary politics still identify concentrated wealth as the principal target.[14] The rise of huge conglomerate corporations and the spread of giant multinationals around the globe have evoked classic populist fears of exploitation. This response has led to probing analyses of both domestic and defense policy in an effort to expose webs of influence and the self-serving policies that result.[15]

Both the populism of the Left and that of the Right play to conspiracy theories of how the United States is "run." The Left highlights links between corporations and the military, while the Right is more concerned with the collusion of powerful bureaucrats and their supporters among the leadership of labor, intellectuals, and other groups identified as having suspect values. Sometimes both ends of the spectrum share common theories of conspiracy, as in the reaction to the reports of the Trilateral Commission. The Commission, initiated by powerful banker David Rockefeller, brought together governmental, corporate, labor, and academic leaders from the United States, Europe, and Japan to fashion a common strategy for approaching the economic and political problems of the capitalist powers. The exercise of influence by these and other elite groups, such as the New York–based Council on Foreign Relations, arouses the suspicion that popular sentiment is being ignored in favor of enhancing the power and profits of insiders.[16]

Populism gave to reform liberalism a whole range of meanings for the concept of positive liberty.[17] By identifying concentrations of private and public power as threats to the interests of the common person, populists put the spotlight on crucial areas for reform. Yet populism and reform liberalism are not identical, for reform liberalism has elements of elitism in its approach to politics that are counter to the democratic radicalism found in the populist movement. Where those elitist tendencies came from is, in part, the story of what the progressive movement added to the development of reform liberalism.

From Progressivism to the New Deal

Populism reached its peak as a visible political movement in the 1890s and thereafter became part of the mainstream through the adoption of some of its programs by the major parties. The progressives rose to prominence just after the turn of the twentieth century and were best known through the presidential candidacies of Theodore Roosevelt in 1912 and Wisconsin Senator Robert LaFollette in 1924. While parties identified with the label *progressive* rose and fell, the movement was carried along on a broad stream of support in many states and cities where progressive ideas and officeholders were responsible for ambitious programs of reform.

Progressivism is a curiously American phenomenon. In a society that lacked a feudal history, a new kind of class system eventuated in which a middle class of independent farmers, shopkeepers, craftsmen, intellectuals, and white-collar salaried employees became a decisive force in American politics. The interests of these people centered on the creation of a rational, orderly, honest society in which hard work would be rewarded and misfortunes could be overcome with the proper assistance. They found their target in abuses of the economic system through fraud and monopolies, and the corruption of government through graft and bossism. Progressives led the attack on both while developing a theory that government could be used to make capitalism work in a more equitable fashion.

William Appleman Williams identifies two broad themes in the program of the progressives: "They wanted to hold the large corporation at its existing level of power while raising other groups to positions of relative balance. They also sought minimum standards of equity and moral behavior."[18] This program appealed to vast sections of American opinion. Rejecting socialist designs for governmental control of the economy, progressives instead supported regulation to eliminate economic abuses such as monopolies, price-fixing, and the exploitation of child labor. Angered at the role of big-city bosses in controlling the nomination of state and national officeholders, Robert LaFollette led a crusade for the establishment of open primaries in which nominees could be selected by the voters. Progressive journalists exposed bribery and graft in government and crooked and inhumane practices by businessmen.

The progressives' passion for clean government led them away from the customary ward politics of city machines and even fostered an aversion to party politics in the usual sense. Progressives believed in the independent expert, accountable only indirectly to public opinion and not at all to the political party leaders. The city-manager form of government, the independent regulatory commission, and the professionalized civil service were all favorite proposals of the progressives. The objective was efficient government free of the tainted influences of wealth and political bossism.

Progressives differed from populists in that they were not believers in radical forms of democracy. The use of expertise borrowed from the universities and the professions in the service of "good government" set progressivism on a course that would lead to accusations of bureaucratic elitism. Whereas Robert LaFollette campaigned vigorously to establish the primary election, he opposed the populist idea of the "initiative"—a form of direct lawmaking by the electorate.[19] LaFollette, along with most other progressives, believed that enlightened leadership was vital and that too much democracy would lead to demagoguery and bad policy. LaFollette stated in his election campaigns, "A vote for me is a vote for the full expression of your views." This assurance meant that he and the progressive leadership would act on behalf of everyone's best interest, which was assumed to lie in rational, well-planned, and honestly executed public policy.

Critics on the Right saw progressives as meddlesome do-gooders who would stifle free enterprise. Big-city liberal politicians saw progressives as moralists who did not understand the realities of urban life, with its need for accommodation and tolerance of diverse lifestyles.[20] Critics on the Left were wary of the middle-class bias of progressive policies, the limited scope of their goals, and the elitism of its leaders. Yet temporary alliances between progressives, urban liberals, and socialists were responsible for major policy initiatives on behalf of the disadvantaged. William Appleman Williams points out that the progressives

> were largely interest-conscious leaders united in a loose, and often mutually suspicious, alliance to check the dominant interest. Their greatest weakness was their lack of any broad and dynamic conception of how the system was to be coordinated and sustained. They did not like the large corporation but they did not have anything to put in its place.[21]

Progressivism led to a patchwork of reforms and a mixed record of accomplishment. Most important, however, progressives, along with urban liberals and labor leaders, established models of governmental intervention in the economy that provided patterns for the New Deal as President Franklin Roosevelt struggled to get the country back on its feet during the Great Depression.[22] The other principal legacy of the progressives was the idea that political reform meant opening the parties up to public inspection and participation. Both sets of ideas provided the agenda for the Democratic Party as it advanced new approaches to positive liberty from the New Deal through the Great Society.

Yet reform liberalism is distinct from progressivism. The New Deal adopted progressive notions of governmental agencies employing experts to address problems of the economy, but those agencies were dismantled by Congress just before the Second World War. The bureaucratic costs did not seem to be justified by the poor performance in rescuing the U.S. economy from the effects of the Depression. It was the massive governmental expenditures of the Second World War that brought the economy around. The relatively small-scale projects of well-motivated experts could not bring sufficient resources to bear on the problems. Progressive notions concerning the government's intervention in the economy were revived after the Second World War, but more significant were initiatives to create large-scale public employment programs and to implement price controls. The progressive style of reform was more successful, as we shall see, in areas of national policy that used expertise and bureaucracy to attack social ills rather than fundamental economic problems.

From the Fair Deal to the New Frontier

The Fair Deal was President Harry Truman's (1945–1953) label for his program of domestic activism on behalf of workers and farmers disadvantaged by postwar economic changes. The New Frontier was President John Kennedy's (1961–1963) phrase for a revival of reform liberalism in limited areas of public policy. As illustrations of reform liberal ideology, the limitations and failures of these programs are as instructive as their successes.

The most dramatic breakthroughs of reform liberals during both administrations concerned civil liberties. Racial discrimination became a high-priority concern of the Democratic Party in 1948 when Mayor Hubert Humphrey of Minneapolis led a walk-out from the Democratic National Convention to protest segregationist practices by Democratic parties in southern states. Although the Truman administration had integrated the armed forces, it otherwise proceeded slowly in confronting institutionalized racism in the United States. Reform liberals wanted the government to take an active role by using constitutional reform and federal law to undermine the legal framework of segregation. In the period between the two administrations, the modern civil rights movement gained momentum under the leadership of Rev. Martin Luther King (see Chapter Eight). This movement forced President Kennedy to raise civil rights to the top of his agenda and to declare that "race has no place in American life or law."[23] Implementing this policy ultimately required the use of federal lawyers, voting registrars, and even troops. Southern governors, mayors, and sheriffs confronted federal efforts to enforce the rights of blacks to attend educational institutions and use other public facilities. Reform liberalism was enormously strengthened by its successes in breaching the barriers of legalized segregation.

In a second respect, the two administrations were similar in their approach to reform liberalism. The goals of foreign policy were shaped by both Truman and Kennedy out of a determination to confront Russian and Chinese threats to U.S. interests. Communism is opposed by reform liberals precisely because it violates individual freedoms that are at the heart of the liberal creed. Both administrations did not shrink from direct confrontations with communist military overtures such as occurred in Korea and Cuba. However, both presidents tried to use constructive means of defusing the appeal of communism: the Marshall Plan under Truman offered generous assistance to war-damaged nations in Europe, and Kennedy's Alliance for Progress was aimed at appealing to progressive forces in Latin America. Liberal capitalism could confront communism through appeals to reason, idealism, and economic self-interest, backed up by force when necessary. The reliance on force ultimately led reform liberals into an uneasy alliance with the growing power of the military-industrial complex throughout the Cold War of the fifties and on into Vietnam in the sixties and seventies.

What was unsuccessful in the Truman and Kennedy administrations were proposals such as those contained in the Full Employment Act of 1946 for a form of national economic planning to secure jobs for the unemployed, if necessary through government-directed work programs. Price controls were similarly unpopular. Blocked by conservatives from using job programs to secure opportunity for the disadvantaged, reform liberals relied on economic growth, some of it financed by escalating military budgets, and economic regulation, occasionally including attempts at price and wage controls.

The Great Society

With the assassination of John Kennedy in 1963, Lyndon B. Johnson became president of the United States (1963–1969). Raised in rural Texas, where reform liberalism had meant roads, rural electrification, and water projects during the thirties, Johnson transformed a wave of sympathy for Kennedy into support for a broad agenda of reform liberal programs.

Prodded by the increasing militancy of the civil rights movement, Johnson pushed legislation to outlaw discrimination in voting, public accommodations, education, and employment. He extended the concept of the Peace Corps to a domestic version, Vista, designed to deal with poverty at home. Community assistance programs were established to channel resources to urban reform groups independently of the political machines that restricted the power and prospects of poor people. Education received huge new subsidies; health care was opened up to public insurance and regulation; social agencies were expanded to deal with the complex needs of the poor; and basic subsistence benefits were increased. The theme of all of these efforts was active assistance to those in need of counseling, education, health care, income maintenance and, to a limited extent, employment.

The failure to expand the Great Society into an effective program for providing public employment to the disadvantaged was largely attributable to the Vietnam War. The reform liberal style of using carefully rationalized incremental responses to the war in Indochina led to an ever-escalating commitment of money and troops. Yet the conflict was based in decades of struggle by the Vietnamese to throw foreigners out of their country. It was a confrontation of technical expertise by raw nationalism that the United States, like France before it, could not comprehend. The war siphoned off money and support that might have made the Great Society more effective.[24] The same problem of limited scale that prevented a full test of New Deal reforms restricted the impact of the Great Society.

The Decline of Reform Liberalism

The swirling currents of politics in the 1970s saw the furthest advances of governmental activism and finally the beginning of a broad-scale retreat. The increasing cost of military budgets, the economic impact of rapidly escalating energy prices, and the deepseated nature of many social problems cast a shadow on Great Society programs. But the essential problem that was not solved was how to move the reform liberal agenda into serious involvement in the distributive characteristics of the economy.

The furthest advance of redistributive policies came, paradoxically, in the Nixon administration with the failure of the Family Assistance Plan (FAP). FAP represented the culmination of a campaign to get traditional conservatives to agree with liberals that welfare should be placed on a national footing along with Social Security as a part of the nation's basic "safety net." Moving the responsibility for welfare from the states to the federal government permitted the vast disparities between states in the level of support and the fairness of administration to be addressed. The Nixon administration, however, withdrew its support in the face of opposition led by Governor Ronald Reagan of California.[25]

The relationship of reform liberalism to welfare programs is more complex than it may appear. Reform liberals have historically stopped short of equalizing income for its own sake and have generally preferred government programs that offer education and other indirect forms of assistance rather than a hand-out. However, basic income maintenance for those least able to take care of themselves is seen as essential. Traditional conservatives also believe in basic support for the indigent. The definition of basic need is the key question, and reform liberals have a different answer from that of traditional conservatives.

Publicly provided welfare originated as a replacement for private charity. From the beginning, it was linked to conservative notions of the management of the lifestyles of its recipients. All the dominant social institutions made their mark: the family through the regulations associated with Aid to Families with Dependent Children; business institutions through regulations on employment; the church through regulations on personal behavior.

The conservative objective is generally to reserve welfare for fatherless families of unemployable women and their children. Employable males are to be excluded, cohabitation for women on welfare is forbidden, and income from part-time jobs is sharply restricted. Reform liberals, beginning with Social Security for older citizens, attempted to broaden the notion of welfare so that it became a matter of right for any person falling below a certain income level. Libertarian conservatives opposed government-sponsored welfare programs for all but the most extreme cases, preferring instead to force self-reliance. Where that fails, private charity is the answer.

The maintenance of a basic income was seen by reform liberals as a prerequisite for entrance into competition for a decent standard of living. The use of welfare to regulate personal behavior was resisted and eligibility restrictions loosened. Liberals and conservatives could agree on "categorical" aid programs to the handicapped and the retarded; however, reform liberals worked toward a concept of minimum income as a basic right. It was this movement that began to fade with the defeat of the Family Assistance Plan, and with it came the beginning of the end of reform liberal ascendancy. The first major victory of contemporary conservatism over reform liberalism was the defeat of the Family Assistance Plan, and this opened the way for a broader assault in the presidential elections of 1976 and 1980.

Bureaucracy and larger budgets for social expenditures were the handmaidens of the implementation of the reform liberal agenda. Both attracted increasing fire from conservatives and those who resented the redistribution of opportunity, income, and power to the disadvantaged and to the public and private agencies whose programs assisted them. Libertarian conservatives feared the concentration of power in government. Traditional conservatives were caught with a dilemma: if welfare was restricted to fatherless families, as it should be to enforce male job-seeking, it encouraged fatherless families, a moral and social danger. Welfare programs were, in this sense, designed to fail politically, while not really addressing the basic needs of the poor for jobs, upward mobility, and the possibility of competing successfully.

Modest reforms of the welfare system failed to attract congressional support during the Carter administration (1977–1981), as did efforts to establish large-scale publicly funded job programs. The reform liberal agenda did advance in the area of environmental protection. New initiatives were taken toward ensuring equal rights for women, minorities, gays, and the handicapped. In this respect, reform liberals were adding to their program ideas gained from the liberation ideologies (see Chapter Eight).

With the election of Ronald Reagan to the presidency in 1980, a broad tide of reaction moved against the reform liberals. Social spending was targeted as the cause of deficits and disappointing economic performance. While government spending and deficits increased due to military expenditures, domestic budgets were sharply curtailed and many social programs were eliminated. The enforcement of environmental and civil rights legislation was slackened and unions were forced to make concessions.

Tax cuts became the advertised method of advancing economic growth and stimulating employment, rather than direct governmental assistance. Cuts in domestic expenditures, increased military budgets, and foreign borrowing to finance historic levels of deficit spending contributed greatly to reducing inflation and improving economic indicators, some decrease in unemployment, and higher levels of poverty. Reform liberal initiatives for positive liberty began to be abandoned as the Democratic Party puzzled over how to renovate reform liberalism in this new political environment.

■ Conclusion

Reform liberalism remains a synthesis of many strands in American politics. It presents the alternative to a straightforward reliance on the vicissitudes of the marketplace as the arbiter of national life. Yet the favorite means of addressing this problem—governmental action—has become increasingly controversial. The direct expense of poverty programs is more visible than the social costs of deprivation. Subsidies to the disadvantaged are more obvious than subsidies to the middle class and the beneficiaries of government contracts. The liberalization of norms of personal behavior has become associated in the public mind with the social consequences of welfare programs. The creation of a class of dependent citizens runs counter both to individualist values and to the original desire of reform liberals to enable all people to participate effectively in a market society.

Reform liberalism may be revived in its historical form as inequalities once again become a center of public concern. There is little else in prospect as a political response to the tendency of capitalism to produce great inequality of result. Much less likely, given the American experience, would be the emergence of the kind of socialist alternative found in other industrialized countries.

■ Notes

[1]As Theda Skocpol points out, the choice of "liberal" as the name for Roosevelt's programs was deliberate: it was meant to appeal to progressives while keeping a safe distance from socialists. Although Skocpol uses Samuel Beer's term, "practical liberalism," for this program, she describes it as "reformist" in every respect. The direction of the reforms clearly changed the institutional thrust of liberalism toward more government and was seen to be practical only in comparison with socialism and progressivism, not previous versions of liberalism per se. See Theda Skocpol, "The Legacies of New Deal Liberalism," in Douglas MacLean and Claudia Mills, eds., *Liberalism Reconsidered* (Totowa, N.J.: Rowman and Allenhead, 1983), pp. 87–104. Though differently defined, the phrase fits generally with the usage by Kenneth Dolbeare and Patricia Dolbeare in *American Ideologies: The Competing Political Beliefs of the 1970s*, 3rd ed. (Chicago: Rand McNally, 1976), p. 72 ff.

[2]The debate that rages on whether the reduction of inequality is possible is analyzed from a reform liberal point of view by Philip Green in *The Pursuit of Inequality* (New York: Random House, 1981).

[3]Benjamin Franklin put it very clearly: "The Combinations of Civil Society are not like those of a Set of Merchants, who club their Property in different Proportions for Building and Freighting a Ship, and may therefore have some Right to vote in disposition of the Voyage in a greater or less Degree according to their respective Contributions; but the important ends of Civil Society, and the personal Secur-

ities of Life and Liberty, these remain the same in every Member of the society; and the poorest continues to have an equal Claim to them with the most opulent, whatever Difference Time, Chance, or Industry may occasion in their Circumstances." In *Writings of Benjamin Franklin*, ed. by Albert Smyth (Haskell), vol. X, pp. 58–60. Cited in Staughton Lynd, *The Intellectual Origins of American Radicalism* (Cambridge, Mass.: Harvard University Press, 1982), p. 71.

[4]This analysis is pursued in detail by Lynd, op. cit., pp. 20, 67–90. Cf. Dumas Malone, *Jefferson the Virginian* (Boston: Little, Brown, 1948), pp. 227–228; Carl Becker, *The Declaration of Independence* (New York: Vintage, 1958).

[5]Lynd, op. cit., pp. 76–77, 83.

[6]In the first version of the Wisconsin Constitution for example, the chartering of banks was expressly *forbidden* because of anger over currency swindles by frontier bankers. See Robert Nesbit, *Wisconsin: A History* (Madison: University of Wisconsin Press, 1973).

[7]For a discussion of the repression of these movements, see Alan Wolfe, *The Seamy Side of Democracy* (New York: David McKay, 1973), especially pp. 120–121.

[8]John Diggins, *The American Left in the Twentieth Century* (New York: Harcourt Brace Jovanovich, 1973), p. 41.

[9]In North Dakota, a populist governor in the early 1920s succeeded in establishing a state-run bank that exists to this day.

[10]For a comprehensive history of populism, see Lawrence Goodwyn, *Democratic Promise: The Populist Movement in America* (New York: Oxford University Press, 1976).

[11]George B. Tindall, *A Populist Reader: Selections from the Works of American Populist Leaders* (New York: Harper, 1966), p. xv.

[12]See Irving Kristol, "The New Populism: Not to Worry," *The Wall Street Journal*, July 25, 1985.

[13]See Richard Viguerie, *The Establishment Vs. the People: Is a New Populist Revolt on the Way?* (Chicago: Regnery Gateway, 1983).

[14]See Jack Greenfield and Jeff Newfield, *A Populist Manifesto* (New York: Praeger, 1972).

[15]See, for example, Kenneth Dolbeare, *Democracy at Risk: The Politics of Economic Renewal* (Chatham, N.J.: Chatham House, 1984) and Richard Barnet, *The Roots of War* (New York: Atheneum, 1972).

[16]For an example of this analysis from the Left, see Holly Sklar, *Trilateralism: The Trilateral Commission and Elite Planning for World Management* (Boston: South End Press, 1980).

[17]A history of these struggles is provided by Howard Zinn, *A People's History of the United States* (New York: Harper & Row, 1981).

[18]William Appleman Williams, *The Contours of American History* (Chicago: Quadrangle Books, 1966), p. 396.

[19]A proposed law is placed on the ballot by petition, and if it passes it takes effect without governmental action. Several states, including California, permit the initiative.

[20]For an account of the relationship of progressivism to urban liberalism, see John Buenker, *Urban Liberalism and Progressive Reform* (New York: Norton, 1974).

[21]Williams, op. cit., p. 396.

[22]A case study in the relationship between progressivism and the New Deal in the area of economic reform is provided by Melvin Urofsky in *A Mind of One Piece: Brandeis and American Reform* (New York: Scribners, 1971). For a survey of other sources, see John Buenker and Nicholas Burckel, eds., *Progressive Reform: A Guide to Information Sources* (Detroit, Michigan: Gale Research Company, 1981).

[23]Cited in Stephen Oates, *Let the Trumpet Sound: The Life of Martin Luther King* (New York: Mentor, 1982), p. 238.

[24]Whether the Great Society succeeded or failed is widely debated; however, poverty levels decreased markedly. See John Schwarz, *America's Hidden Success: A Reassessment of Twenty Years of Public Policy* (New York: Norton, 1983).

[25]Daniel Patrick Moynihan, *The Politics of a Guaranteed Income* (New York: Vintage, 1973), pp. 374–375. Cf. Christopher Leman, *The Collapse of Welfare Reform* (Cambridge, Mass.: MIT Press, 1980), p. 92; Lou Cannon, *Reagan,* (New York: Putnams, 1982), pp. 178–79.

SIX

A spider conducts operations that resemble those of a weaver, and a bee puts to shame many an architect in the construction of her cells. But what distinguishes the worst architect from the best of bees is this, that the architect erects his structure in imagination before he erects it in "reality."

Karl Marx
Capital, Volume I (1867)

Marxism

Karl Marx (1818–1883) did not invent communism. The idea of people living and working cooperatively has a long history. Significant communal utopias can be found in the literature of the Greeks, the early Christians, the monastics, and seventeenth-century English rebels against the institutionalization of private property.[1] Though his vision of communism may not have been original, Marx's distinctive achievement was a theory of how communism would come about—a development he advocated with intellectual skill and enormous energy.

Marx was a critic of classical liberalism. The targets of his impassioned writings were those who saw individual self-interest as the fundamental principle of society. He thought that human beings had a purpose quite different from the simple fulfillment of appetites or the pursuit of vanity as described in the theory of Adam Smith. Marx forecast that a society based on the laissez faire principle of separating politics from economics would be class-ridden and subject to ultimate collapse.

As with other ideologies, Marxism proceeds from a view of the human condition to an analysis of politics. Karl Marx's conception of the human condition begins with a fundamental question: what is the difference between human beings and lower animals? From his answer to the question, Marx constructs an entire theory of the purpose of human life and the meaning of history. He also creates his scenario for explaining how this purpose might guide the development of new forms of politics and community life. Marx's imagery is compelling because it touches on basic human aspirations.

In the first section, we will preview the image Marx had of what life could be like in a society where true humanity is achieved and people live together as he thinks they are meant to. In the next section, we will explore the framework of Marx's analysis of capitalism and outline the steps that were to lead to communism.

■ *Marx's Vision of Communism*

Like all other powerful philosophies, Marxism is based on an analysis of human nature. To the question about the difference between human beings and lower animals, Marx answers that it isn't just the human capacity for thought or for communication that sets human beings apart—as we know, animals have similar skills. He says that *human beings, unlike animals, are capable of conscious production.* People can transform one thing into another by choice. We can combine coal and iron to make steel. With steel we can create a sword or a plowshare. Animals, by contrast, produce only in response to instinct or accidental variations of previously learned patterns. Bees and spiders can build structures, but not consciously in the way that an architect chooses from alternative designs and fits materials to a plan.

The force that drives human history is the urge each person has to express a potential for conscious production, whether physical or mental. Yet we are held down by class domination that channels some to boring, repetitive jobs and others to lives of ease and leisure. Human potential is stifled by the inequality and injustice of a world that is not yet organized to maximize conscious production. Instead we spend our working lives, for the most part, in forms of production, whether physical or mental, that offer us little choice about what we do or how it is done. The requirements of survival force people to work merely to serve basic needs. Work of this kind is a far cry from the expression of an inner urge to develop individual talents and creative possibilities.

Marx traces the historical evolution of the human species through various forms of society. He wants to see how the species struggles to realize its true nature. Marx was a contemporary of Charles Darwin and admired the way that Darwin had separated the study of nature from theological conceptions of the creation.[2] Karl Marx's theory is constructed in a manner similar to Darwin's; however, Marx replaces Darwin's notions of competition and natural selection with a dynamic view of human action as the agency of change. Marx wanted to show how history changed as a result of human intervention in the creation of new forms of production and community life. He extracts from this study a pattern to history that can be projected into the future of the species.[3]

Marx views communism as a society having everything in place for a life of maximum conscious productivity. First of all, basic needs for food, shelter, and clothing would be provided by the community. Goods and services would be produced in a way that does not consume all our productive energy or destroy the motivation to be creative. Marx also spells out why attitudes would change so that people would willingly participate in such a system: everyone would work together for part of the present workday—say, three or four hours—at some socially necessary task.

How could basic needs be supplied in such a short workday? By a cooperative approach to the production of necessities, people would learn to work together for the common good. If production were organized so as to match individual abilities to the type of work, foster democratic techniques of planning, and remove the profit motive, the work done for necessity would be humanized. Eliminating the waste associated with competition, the frustrations of boring jobs, and the anger arising from relations of domination would make communal production much more efficient. The creation of new technology would further reduce the need for drudgery.

Through work organized in this way, individuals would be entitled to receive the necessities of life. They would simultaneously be learning the attitudes appropriate to cooperative living. Capitalism drives people apart through competition, manipulation, and domination. The rational organization of production would overcome personal alienation and depression and permit the fulfillment of people's true social potential.

The maxim that would guide production and distribution in this "realm of necessity" would be: "From each according to his ability, to each according to his need."[4] Individuals would receive from the community whatever was needed to support their particular contribution to the society. The work devoted to producing necessities would be the ticket to a life where one would not have to worry about basic needs. Marx appears to argue that without participation in such work, an individual would not be entitled to the benefits of communism.

To satisfy basic needs is not to fulfill entirely the purpose of life. It is only a preliminary condition to a life in which true humanity might emerge. In organizing production in the realm of necessity by these principles, Marx says we will be freed of the dog-eat-dog struggle for survival, the boredom of specialization, and the pressures of competition that detract from a person's humanity. Theoretically, the efficiencies gained by this means would enable production to keep up with expanding social needs as new techniques and products for the improvement of life are invented. The enhanced quality of human interaction would make possible a more considerate approach to personal growth, social life, and the environment.

How does this happen? The answer, again, has to do with the proper human relationship to production. The fulfillment of the vision of communism is in what happens not in the *realm of necessity* but in the *realm of freedom*. The realm of freedom is where the promise of conscious production is fulfilled. It is that part of the day when people can produce whatever their abilities and interests allow without concern for supplying necessities.

Those who are used to the kind of work that Marx describes as alienating might think that this "free time" would be spent in idle pursuits, sleep, and general time-wasting. Marx doesn't think so. Here is where true conscious productivity would manifest itself. Individuals would find the chance to express previously suppressed interests: to perfect various skills, make more refined products, and challenge the boundaries of knowledge or achievement in a field of endeavor. Free rein would be given to intellectual curiosity and creative impulses. A librarian might learn to become a doctor. A doctor might learn to make furniture. Manual skills would no longer be divided from intellectual skills; people would have the freedom and the encouragement to develop both.

Why wouldn't people do the minimum and simply idle away the rest of the time? Marx's fundamental assumption about human creativity comes into play here. When people do crossword puzzles, they become bored with simple versions and move on to greater challenges. Hobbyists try to refine their techniques. Athletes aim for ever higher levels of performance even when the competition is entirely voluntary. The human desire for expression and accomplishment will lead people to produce in an ever more interesting and creative fashion.

With the advance of communism, production would flourish. Rather than the gray, routinized social prison described by its detractors, Marx suggests that communism offers dazzling possibilities. Creativity would be liberated from exploitation. "Free" productivity might well become the dominant source of goods and services as individuals advance old skills and crafts and invent new ones. A plenitude of ideas would stimulate fresh waves of productive energy, new technologies, and innovations of all kinds. Work would be valued for its human qualities rather than as simply a means to survival.

This vision of an egalitarian society of freely producing individuals is among the great utopias of Western political thought.[5] It has enormous power as a political symbol for movements the world over. The story of how this utopia might come into being is rather complicated and requires a study of Marx's framework for the analysis of history.

■ *Analysis of Marx's Theory*

Understanding Marx's ideas is a special challenge for people raised in capitalist societies. Much education and socialization have been directed toward discrediting Marxism. Few students will ever have heard a discussion of Marx in his own terms.

Marx must be held at least partly responsible for the atrocities committed in the name of his theories by Stalin, Mao Tse Tung, and other "Marxist" leaders. However, as we shall see, there is some reason to believe that he would not accept much of what these leaders have done as an expression of Marxism. Furthermore, Marx's influence extends far beyond the U.S.S.R., with dozens of variations on his ideas to be found in the politics of Europe, Africa, Asia, and Latin America. There is, as well, an historically independent tradition of democratic socialism, with which Marxism is sometimes confused. For all these reasons, it is hard to arrive at a clear view of Marx.

A subtler problem in understanding Marx is that we are used to the specialization of knowledge. Universities are usually organized into departments of political science, economics, history, philosophy, and so forth. Each specialization separates one body of knowledge from another. Marx was a comprehensive thinker. His system of ideas reaches into all these fields plus many more, such as sociology and anthropology, and even art, religion, and literature.[6] Marx tries to approach the human experience in the same way that we live it: as an integrated whole.

The key to solving some of these problems of understanding is to try to suspend one's preconceptions about his ideas and simply approach them afresh. It is important to try to understand the ideas in their own terms and then to apply critical judgment to the key assumptions, concepts, and evidence. A critique, or a belief, based on faulty understanding accomplishes little except the reinforcement of bias.

Marx explains most of what he has to say in the form of a scenario about the way human history has unfolded and is likely to develop in the future. Following the main elements of this story makes it fairly easy to grasp Marx's basic concepts. Once these concepts have been made clear, the work of analysis and criticism can begin.

To understand something about Marxism is not necessarily to understand the variety of ideas that are bound up in communist parties and movements around the world. Like Christianity or liberalism or any other living tradition, contemporary communism contains new and old streams of interpretation, analysis, and innovation. For introductory purposes, however, Marxism provides the ideological core of communism.

The History of the Species According to Marx

Marx starts from the assumption that the process of production shapes our lives. Production is both a means to survival and the key to human nature. Whereas history is usually presented as an account of explorations, wars, and the rise and fall of rulers, Marx's version of history centers on developments in how people go about producing to fulfill needs and wants.

Were the history of production simply the story of new inventions to make work more efficient, Marx's history would recount one technical development after another. But that version of history wouldn't explain the conflicts, the rebellions, and the wars that make history so dramatic. Marx points out that production is not just tools and raw materials; it also involves the way people are organized to do the work.

From the organization of production come class structures. For example, as capitalism develops, two classes emerge: the bourgeoisie and the proletariat. The one (bourgeoisie) owns and controls the *means* by which the other (proletariat) makes its living. These two classes have quite different interests: the bourgeoisie is interested in profiting from the labor of others, and the proletariat is interested in survival. The difference between what workers are paid and the value they produce is the principal means by which capitalists gain their profits. Yet, for the workers, wages are the means of their survival.

In capitalism, the owners of the means of production, the bourgeoisie, are the dominant class in the government as well as in the economy. Where they do not rule directly through officials appointed or elected from their ranks, they rule indirectly by shaping the views and beliefs, the opportunities and career paths of those who do rule. Even if a working-class person ascends to a position of power, following the interests of the bourgeoisie is a condition of maintaining influence.

It is this relation of domination between classes that accounts for the major conflicts in history. As new technologies change the possibilities for organizing production, the old ruling class fights off new challengers. For example, in the middle of the eighteenth century, the Yankee mill owners who mechanized textile production were no longer interested in being subjected to the political power of the southern aristocracy. In the Marxist version of what happened in the U.S. Civil War, the plantation owners battled the northern mill owners. Southern plantation owners tried to preserve a class system based in slavery against the rise of a new order built on an alliance between Yankee industrialists and small midwestern farmers who did not enjoy competing with inexpensive slave labor. These real conflicts of economic interest were at the root of the Civil War, rather than lofty principles of human freedom.

In Marx's terminology, the reason for conflict is that the *relations of production* (the class system by which production is organized) change more slowly than the *means of production* (technology and raw materials). Demands for new goods and services, as well as human inventiveness, mean that technologies are constantly being refined and the uses of raw materials improved. As these changes occur, they bring with them implications for the way production is organized. The groups losing power under the new arrangements resist change. History is a series of battles on many levels between rising and declining classes.

What makes history so complicated is that class structures pervade *all* the techniques of social control. Among these techniques Marx includes religion, popular political ideas, and even the self-conceptions that people are taught to have. It is cheaper to use ideas to rule people than it is to hire police. Ideas are the velvet glove on the iron fist of power. Class-based control permeates our social and personal environments.[7]

Just as Darwin used the concepts of variation and natural selection to explain evolution, so Marx has a set of basic concepts that are the keys to the dynamics of human history. Marx's scenario will begin to fit together as we examine the meaning of those basic concepts. Then we will see how his fundamental categories are used to explain history. Finally, we can follow the application of these concepts to the task of explaining how history moves from capitalism through socialism to communism.

The Fundamental Categories of Marx's Theory

In order to see these relationships more clearly, it is helpful to simplify Marx's analytical framework. G. V. Plekhanov (1857–1918), a Russian interpreter of Marx, presents Marx's categories for the analysis of a society as follows:

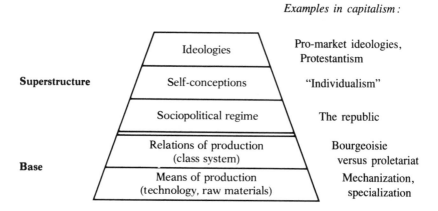

Examples in capitalism:

		Examples in capitalism
Superstructure	Ideologies	Pro-market ideologies, Protestantism
	Self-conceptions	"Individualism"
	Sociopolitical regime	The republic
Base	Relations of production (class system)	Bourgeoisie versus proletariat
	Means of production (technology, raw materials)	Mechanization, specialization

The two elements of the base, the means of production and the relations of production, together shape the superstructure: the government, religion, and the beliefs that people are taught to have about themselves. When the introduction of new means of production generates changed relations of production, the conflict of new and old class structures is fought out through all levels of the superstructure. Rival classes fight over who is to control the government. Religions change. New ideas challenge prevailing self-conceptions.

As an example of how ideas become a method of shaping behavior, consider Marx's view of the "science" of economics as capitalists present it. Economics is thought of as a matter of matching supply and demand. This view places investment and the ownership of the means of production in a central role. Workers become "raw material" as suppliers of labor, rather than human beings with basic needs and a capacity for conscious production. Economists concern themselves with market prices and satisfying the wants of those who have money, rather than with human needs and the way that value is created by laborers and disposed of by capitalists.[8] Idea systems such as modern economics serve the dominant class, according to Marx. That is why they are reinforced in the schools, churches, and workplaces.[9]

Another example of the political use of ideas is Marx's view that the very concept of individualism works against the interests of true personal freedom. Free speech under liberalism becomes the right of the media owner to drown out the voice of the lonely dissenter. Individual ownership of property becomes the justification for huge inequalities in the distribution of wealth. None of these circumstances really allows the individual to be the architect of his or her own destiny. True freedom is based in real changes in the means and relations of production, not airy concepts of individual rights.

Changes in these configurations take decades and even centuries before there are decisive transitions from one historical epoch to another. Marx categorizes human history into periods differentiated by large-scale changes in which the power of a declining class at all levels of society gives way over time to the dominance of a new class; for example, from the feudal reign of princes and popes, to the rise of industrial capitalism, to revolutionary socialism.

The shift between historical epochs can be seen in the rise of political republics, such as took place in Britain in the seventeenth century. The class that controlled the new means of production having to do with trade and commerce came to power through the strengthening of Parliament. The new bourgeoisie confronted the authority of the feudal hierarchy based in the land, and reduced the king to the role of an executive who shares power with Parliament. As the demands of trade and commerce required greater individual mobility, liberal ideas based on individual freedom and economic competition replaced systems of thought that emphasized each person's place in the larger order of things. Protestantism, with its theology of the individual's relationship to God, confronted the Catholicism of the rural aristocracy, with its ties to feudal structures of political and religious power.

All these changes, the conflicts included, are part of the struggle by humanity to realize the inner desire to engage in conscious production. Major historical developments may be traced to the influence of economic changes upon various levels of society. Yet Marx does not mean to say that all of human behavior is determined by narrowly conceived economic factors, as if people had no part in creating their own destiny. His point is that the struggle for free productivity is worked out at many levels, the most powerful of which is the means and relationships of production. Individuals play a role in creating new means of production and in responding to the pressures created by the relationships of production both in their working lives and in the many levels of the superstructure. History is dynamic. People supply the energy, and their need to produce creates patterns in how that dynamic is played out.

The Transition from Capitalism to Socialism

Marx's most famous prediction is that capitalism will crumble and be overthrown, to be replaced by a new socialist order that will prepare the way for true communism. Why will this happen? Marx's answer can be understood by applying the logic of his basic concepts. This done, we will explore Marx's conception of socialism, and finally return to the beginning point of this chapter: Marx's vision of communism.

The fundamental tension in any historical period is in the misfit of the relations of production (the way work is organized) to changes in the means of production (technology and raw materials). That is where we should look to understand Marx's analysis of capitalism. Marx adapts from the philosophy of Georg Friedrich Hegel the notion of a "contradiction" to explain how a society can be at odds with itself. Capitalism, according to Marx, is a mass of contradictions between what the species *wants* by way of conscious productivity and what it *gets* from the capitalist system of organizing production.

The whole objective of management in a capitalist society is to break down complicated jobs into simpler, more specialized tasks.

This approach allows management to minimize wages, cut down on labor time, and ultimately replace workers with machines whenever they can do the work more cheaply. Yet the proletariat, the largest class, exists by selling its labor and using the wages to buy the products of its own labor. How can a system survive that ultimately tries to abolish its own basis for creating wealth? As Marx puts it, the fundamental contradiction of capitalism is that it "presses to reduce labor time to a minimum, while it posits labor time, on the other side, as sole measurement and source of wealth."[10]

Add to this contradiction another one: capitalism creates in its factories the potential for huge enterprises where production *could* take place on a planned and cooperative basis, yet it does so in a way that pits one worker against another in competition. Or yet another: capitalism creates great wealth, but distributes it to very few, while many remain in abject poverty.

All these contradictions present both an advance toward the goal of free productivity and an obstacle to further progress. Minimizing labor time is a good thing. Properly used, it could free everyone for conscious production. The abundance of goods and services brought into being by entrepreneurship is useful in making life easier and more secure. Yet the system forces people into ever more constraining and competitive roles. Cooperative production is a key to the provision of basic needs for all. Yet all of capitalism's achievements come at the price of a class system that benefits the rich and consigns many to spend their lives in a struggle merely to subsist.

So far, nothing has been said about capitalism that hasn't been pointed out by non-Marxist socialists (see Chapter Seven). Marx differs in his analysis in that he sees the change from capitalism to socialism as inevitable. Non-Marxist socialists, sometimes referred to as democratic socialists, generally believe that the change could come about through persuasion and electoral change.[11] Marx believes that it will happen for objective reasons of history and that it will involve revolution.

Marx's objective reasons for thinking that capitalism will fall have to do with the crises created by the contradictions. Two sets of crises will occur: for economic reasons, the rate of profit will decline; and for sociological reasons, the proletariat will become a militant revolutionary force bent on overthrowing capitalism. These two sets of crises bear closer examination.

The Economics of Capitalism's Collapse

Profit is the key to capitalism. From it come investment and the capacity of the system for renewal and expansion. Marx argues that there is an inner logic to capitalism that will ultimately lead to a collapse in the rate of profit. As managers try to minimize labor costs, they will introduce machines. There is a crucial difference between people and machines when it comes to generating profit.

A machine is very simple in economic terms: either one can pay the fixed cost of operating the machine or one can't. Workers are different. There is no fixed cost for labor except the price of human subsistence. A worker may produce a great deal of value but be paid very little as a result of competitive wage rates. The "surplus value," to use Marx's term, comes to the capitalist as profit. Separating the question of *value produced* from *wages paid* creates the potential for the profitable use of labor. The key to profiting from someone else's labor is to persuade or force the worker to accept wages that are lower, perhaps much lower, than the value the worker creates. Machines can't be persuaded or forced; it is either economical to operate the machine or it isn't. A surplus is possible from a machine, but manipulation is not.

Under conditions of competition, the difference between laborers and machines becomes critical. If two manufacturers make the same product on the same machine, competition would force the price of the product down to the cost of operating the machine. The result would be little or no profit. However, if workers rather than machines make the product, there is a chance that profitability can be sustained by separating wages from value.

Even for labor-based production, under pure competition, wage rates could be forced down to the subsistence level. In the absence of unions or price-fixing, the rate of profit might fall with labor-based production as it does with machines. However, machines do not consume their own products, nor can they be misled about the relation between wages and value. So the depressing effect on the rate of profit is speeded up when production becomes mechanized.

Even so, as long as the demand for goods holds up and there is imperfect competition, capitalists can continue to make profits. Profits fall and capitalism gets into trouble due to the cumulative effect of genuine competition in saturated markets, the reduction in the amount of surplus available to workers as purchasing power, and the displacement of workers by machines.

At the very least, Marx clearly underestimated how long it would take for this to happen. Some take the periodic depressions and recessions in capitalist economies as evidence that Marx wasn't completely wrong. It is often observed that government has stepped in to prevent pure competition from occurring. Government has legitimated labor unions, established minimum wages, used tax revenues to prop up failing industries, and subsidized large sectors of the economy through the military-industrial complex.

Meanwhile, entrepreneurs have come up with new products and ways of increasing consumer demand through advertising and the planned obsolescence of cars and other products. These measures are seen by Marxists to have saved the capitalist system from its ultimate crisis. However, if Marx is right, governmental intervention and the expansion of markets have their limits. If markets for basic goods ever become satiated, the contradiction between profit and the minimization of labor time should finally bring the economic collapse of the system.

We have been examining changes in the means of production that are to lead to capitalism's collapse. Yet revolutions do not happen without human action—what will make workers turn toward revolutionary socialism? To answer this, it is necessary to understand the corresponding changes in the relations of production.

Capitalism and Class Conflict

Marx argues that capitalism leads to the increasing exploitation of workers by capitalists. Exploitation has many facets. In addition to extracting surplus value, capitalists try to dominate the cultural environment and even the personal life of workers. Intentionally or not, they make work ever more alienating; and they repress dissent through manipulation and force. Each of these aspects of exploitation rebounds in the form of revolutionary energy as the final crisis of capitalism approaches.

When capitalism matures, Marx argues that the distinction between bourgeoisie and proletariat will become ever clearer. Class differences will intensify. Classes left over from feudalism, such as artisans and professionals of various kinds, will be forced into the twofold class structure of bourgeoisie and proletariat. Class position will increasingly be determined by the ownership and control of the means of production. The owners will be a small class with sharply different interests from the workers. As the rate of profit declines along with real wages, the conflicting nature of these interests will become crystal clear.

Meanwhile, due to the increasingly specialized and routinized character of work under capitalism, workers will become alienated. The concept of alienation is one of Marx's most potent ideas. Alienation means a sense of separation—in this case a separation arising from the difference between what the worker has to do to make a living and the worker's innate desire to engage in conscious production. Alienation arouses feelings of self-hatred, attitudes of distrust toward fellow workers, and generalized anger and escapist behavior.

Marx's vision of communism is one of alienation overcome by the creation of the best possible environment for conscious production. But under capitalism, wage labor is a perversion of conscious production. Workers have no say in what is produced, the design of the product, how the work is performed, or what is done with the results. In the process of wage labor, people are forced to compete with fellow workers rather than cooperating. Personal relationships degenerate into calculations based on self-interest. Alienation at first distracts workers from organizing to solve their problems. Private forms of rebellion and escape substitute for satisfaction at work. Finally alienation becomes so severe that workers are led to common action to redress their situation. Class consciousness begins to develop.

All these processes come to life politically when they are translated into action on behalf of the working class. The formation of class consciousness is the key to action. Marx means by class consciousness an awareness of one's true class position. Prior to the period of revolution, many people assume that their individuality is more important than their class position in determining their lives. Or people may have "false consciousness"—they may think that they are part of the bourgeoisie because they are salaried, or earn a middle-range income, or do "white-collar" work. In fact, they neither own nor control the means by which they make a living.

Perhaps the subtlest barrier to class consciousness is the cultural self-concept of individualism that is so prominent in capitalist societies. When people think of themselves primarily as unique individuals, they become politically confused. They become susceptible to appeals based on emotion, strong leaders, and vague theories of self-improvement. The ideology of classical liberalism, by stressing individualism, plays into the hands of the capitalists, according to Marx. As individuals, the people are a shapeless mass who can be manipulated. As a class conscious of its political mission, the proletariat becomes powerful.

Still, the rise of class consciousness comes only after other factors such as religious divisions, ethnic and racial differences, and regional separation are overcome. Workers must come to realize that nothing shapes their lives so much as their class position. The families of the working poor face a far different set of life chances from those of the inheritors of great wealth, regardless of religious belief, ethnic identity, or region. Capitalists manipulate the differences as a way of keeping the proletariat divided by playing off one race, ethnic group, or regional economic situation against another.

Workers slowly learn to overcome these differences through common action.

The Convergence of Collapse and Class War

When class consciousness takes root and begins to grow through political action, workers will see ever more clearly the true nature of their interests. Workers will begin to understand that they can get back the full value of their labor only if they are in control of the system. They will come out of their alienation into a movement that can seize upon the collapse of capitalism and overthrow the rule of the bourgeoisie.

The objective of the revolution will be the replacement of the capitalist ownership of the means of production by worker ownership through the state. By means of this revolution, the enormous productive power of capitalist industry can be harnessed to the socialist objective of providing everyone with the necessities of life. As the socialist system takes root and replaces capitalism, these tasks can be accomplished by cooperative rather than competitive relations of production.

The creation of a revolutionary situation along the lines of Marx's scenario depends upon the interaction between worsening economic conditions and intensifying sociological factors. It is not enough for the economy to fall apart; class consciousness must also have taken hold. The workers have to see clearly the position they hold in capitalism and the reasons why they are exploited. As the rate of profit falls, workers get squeezed out and their jobs become more routinized and specialized. Their class consciousness must be developed through political action.

Marx sees the revolution approaching through escalating crises:

> Hence the highest development of productive power together with the greatest expansion of existing wealth will coincide with depreciation of capital, degradation of the labourer, and a most straitened exhaustion of his vital powers. . . . These contradictions, of course, lead to explosions, crises, in which momentary suspension of all labour and annihilation of a great part of the capital violently lead it back to the point where it is enabled [to go on] fully employing its productive powers without committing suicide. Yet, these regularly recurring catastrophes lead to their repetition on a higher scale, and finally its violent overthrow.[12]

If there is an economic crisis, but little class consciousness, remedies such as the dictatorial centralization of all power in the state may be the result rather than genuine socialist revolution. Some Marxists see the fascist repression of socialist movements in Germany in the 1930s as an example of this kind of failed revolution. On the other hand, if class consciousness is highly developed and yet capitalism is still healthy, the proletariat may not be strong enough to overcome the forces commanded by capitalists and bring off the revolution. The scenario for revolution can go wrong, but the factors that produce a revolutionary situation will recur so long as capitalism remains.

Building Socialism

The purpose of the revolution is to open the door to the development of a classless society—or more descriptively, a society in which all people share the common tasks of providing necessities. The purpose is to "build socialism" and create the conditions for the transition to communism. The stage of building socialism is quite different from communism itself. Since this is the stage the U.S.S.R. claims to be in, it is particularly important to see how it is supposed to proceed.

The task of building socialism has three major thrusts: the reorientation of economic relations to the socialist mode, the defeat of bourgeois institutions and attitudes, and the construction of a new socialist superstructure affecting all aspects of the society. The factories and offices need to be reorganized along socialist lines so that workers have a controlling voice in how the work is carried on. The production goals must be coordinated to meet the needs of society. This is a huge task, similar to what was done in mobilizing the U.S. economy for our participation in the Second World War.

While the economic base is being reoriented to socialist production, the revolution will have to be defended against attempts by the bourgeoisie to reclaim their power. Marx envisions a revolutionary period followed by subsequent skirmishes and smaller conflicts. The subtler part of the struggle to secure the victory of the proletariat will lie in the battle for people's "hearts and minds." Bourgeois ideas must be attacked and replaced with socialist conceptions. Workers have to see themselves as "comrades" rather than competitors. Religious ideas must not be used to distract people from rebuilding society by promising rewards in the afterlife. Art and culture should make people see the real relations of power and struggle that underlie society. The mission of education is to explain the rationale of the new order.

The directing force for all these changes is to be, in Marx's phrase, the "vanguard of the proletariat." The vanguard comprises those who most thoroughly understand the class struggle, the requirements of revolution, and the necessity for personal discipline in building socialism. Marx refers to the vanguard's role in building socialism as "the dictatorship of the proletariat." Marx did not describe this vanguard or its method of operation very carefully. Some socialists read Marx as arguing that the vanguard might be a majority of the society ruling in the name of the proletariat through the devices of democratic government.[13] However, the prevailing interpretation of who is in the vanguard is shaped by the work of Vladimir Ilyich Lenin (1870–1924), the creator of the Communist Party. For Lenin, only a highly centralized party could discipline the revolution in the service of building socialism.[14]

North Americans are used to voluntary political parties; the Communist Party is a completely different kind of organization. The role of the Communist Party is to implement the revolution at all levels of society: from the factory floor to the highest offices of government. Thus party membership is open only to the truly dedicated and qualified. Building on the notion of the dictatorship of the proletariat, the party under Lenin, and especially under his successor, Joseph Stalin (1879–1953), became an all-pervasive force controlling the lives of Soviet citizens.[15] To purify the party and the revolution, Stalin instigated purges in which hundreds of thousands of people perished.

In practice, the state, acting at the direction of the Communist Party, has assumed the major role in building socialism. State ownership of the means of production has not turned out to be the same as worker ownership. The centralization in the state of the power to transform not just production but all aspects of culture and society has led to results that bear little resemblance to Marx's ideals. If Marx thought that individual rights in capitalism were largely illusory, he would have a hard time justifying the direct violations of workers' rights in virtually every communist country today.

The Transition to Communism

Let's return to Marx's scenario. Once socialism is firmly established, the gradual transition to communism can begin. When the socialized factories and offices are producing efficiently, the proportion of the day devoted to producing necessities can be reduced. Wasteful production of nonessentials will be eliminated through planning. As workers become accustomed to cooperative production, they will be increasingly receptive to socialist ideas about the purpose of society and the need for reforms in education, religion, and culture generally. As a new generation is raised with these ideals in mind, the momentum of the socializing process will increase. A new kind of socialist citizenship will replace the old capitalist individualism.

These changes will lessen the amount of conflict and crime in the society. Inequalities will be dramatically reduced, removing a major motive for theft and other criminal acts. Since the government will no longer have to devote its energies to maintaining capitalist control over the means of production, and the policing of crime will take fewer and fewer resources, the government itself will "wither away." What will remain are planning functions organized so as to respond to the people's priorities. Democracy based on true equality will operate from the ground up in communities, factories, and offices. Planners and managers will be held accountable through elections.

By degrees the phase of building socialism will end and communism will arrive. In the realm of necessity, production will be organized by socialist principles; in the realm of freedom, a plenitude of individual creativity will assure a world full of interest and stimulation. People will approach the attainment of human "species-being" as masters of necessity, conscious producers, and free human beings in the genuine sense. The vision described at the beginning of this chapter will come into focus as human society arrives at its highest level. The basic structure of society needs no further development because human beings have realized their inner natures.

Marx reviews the whole story in a single famous paragraph in Volume III of *Capital*, his masterwork:

> Just as the savage must wrestle with Nature to satisfy his wants, to maintain and reproduce life, so must civilized man, and he must do so in all social formations and under all possible modes of production. With his development this realm of physical necessity expands as a result of his wants, but, at the same time, the forces of production which satisfy these wants also increase. Freedom in this field can only consist in socialized man, the associated producers, rationally regulating their interchange with Nature, bringing it under their common control, instead of being ruled by it as by the blind forces of Nature; and achieving this with the least expenditure of energy and under conditions most favorable to, and worthy of, their human nature. But it nonetheless still remains a realm of necessity. Beyond it begins that development of human energy which is an end in itself, the true realm of freedom, which, however, can blossom forth only with the realm of necessity as its basis. The shortening of the working day is its basic prerequisite.[16]

■ *Conclusion*

This scenario for the development of communism Marx sometimes saw as inevitable, although he also foresaw that there could be false starts when the key elements were not all in place and a revolution could fail. Many of his historical writings analyze the relationship of key factors in struggles such as the French Revolution, the American Civil War, and nineteenth-century English society.

Lenin took Marx's ideas and fashioned them into a rationale for revolution in the U.S.S.R. Some Marxists point out that Russia was neither capitalist nor industrialized nor even a nation in some respects in 1917. It was, in this view, a vast collection of more than a hundred nationalities and ethnic groups governed by a feudal czarist regime that collapsed under the pressures of the First World War. In the confusion, a small, disciplined, brilliantly led communist minority was able to take over and implement a revolution.

The problem was that capitalism hadn't completed its work of building up the productive base. So that had to be done by force while at the same time finishing with the First World War and repelling invaders from the capitalist nations (the Americans and the British in 1921 during the Russian Civil War, and the Germans again in 1940). The result was a ruthless totalitarian dictatorship that has begun to moderate only recently, leaving its people stultified and its economy woefully inefficient. The Soviets have tacitly acknowledged the difficulty of following Marx's scenario. In 1961, they enacted a plan that was to deliver the Soviet Union to communism beginning in 1980. In 1985, with that goal unattained, the new planning document set no date, but called for "advances" on all fronts.

China is seen as another example of a peasant economy vaulted into socialism without industrialization through the wartime collapse of a corrupted capitalist structure. Today China flirts with competitive relationships of production in order to stimulate the kind of economic development that is so hard to achieve through force. Marx's scenario depends upon an abundance of production to provide for social needs. Neither economy has achieved it.

Although the U.S.S.R. and China can be seen as deviants from the Marxist scenario, it is also true that there is no clear example of a nation that has followed the script. Variations on Marxism have been tried in many developing countries. The results in some countries have been interesting, in others tragic. Virtually all European countries have adapted socialist ideas to their politics, although those ideas have come out of the democratic socialist tradition more often than Marxism.

The United States seems to represent the clearest refutation of the scenario. Capitalism has suffered its economic crises, and it is revealing to use Marx's categories to analyze them, but it has survived and spread prosperity to millions. There is a largely submerged history of Marxist thought and political action in the

United States, but it hasn't succeeded in achieving a mass basis. Class consciousness is a factor in Republican and Democratic politics, but it has been overshadowed by a general consensus on free enterprise as the best way to organize the economy.

Marxists, on the other hand, point to the unique character of the United States as essentially a new nation possessed of abundant resources, with a working class divided by region, race, ethnicity, and sex, so that class consciousness develops only slowly. Moreover, serious economic crises have been met by governmental action to prop up the economy. Governmental intervention and the development of unions that have saved workers from the worst aspects of capitalist competition have retarded the movement toward revolution, in the Marxist view.

Contemporary Marxist thinkers have moved away from the lock-step interpretation of Marx's scenario for the arrival of communism. They have concentrated on interpreting the subtleties and dynamics of class conflict and the functioning of the state in highly complex Western societies.[17] Marx is used as a guide to understanding the strategies of competing interests more often than as the authority on the timetable for revolution.

Although Marx's recipe for class warfare and revolution remains unpopular, his critique of capitalism continues to appeal to those who are concerned about the inequalities, crime, and materialism that seem to accompany capitalist development. Marx is important to modern politics because he still defines a major alternative to the market-based society. Serious political discussions almost anywhere resolve into a comparison of Marxist, democratic socialist, and capitalist approaches to problems and possibilities.

The critical judgment of Marx depends upon analyzing his fundamental assumptions and the connections to his theory of revolution. Is it true that human beings are destined to struggle toward achieving a world in which conscious production can be maximized for all and necessity is reduced to a minimum? In this prophecy lies the almost mystical appeal of his doctrine, and from it flows the analytical ideas that make Marx such a potent critic of capitalism. Or is his model of human nature either inaccurate or too simple? Are there other aspects of human nature that have to be taken into account besides the relationship to production?

If Marx is correct about human nature, is he also correct in his scenario for the downfall of capitalism and the rise of revolutionary communism? Can a revolutionary regime redirect the state toward the implementation of socialism and organize the transition to communism without becoming corrupt and repressive? Is there another path to utopia? Democratic socialists believe there is (see Chapter Seven).

In the century since Marx's death, there has developed a vast body of interpretation that has proposed and sometimes created many variations on Marxist politics. The analysis of these works is beyond the scope of this book; however, all the important variations accept Marx's view of the human condition. They differ primarily over his analysis of how contradictions are worked out within capitalism, the role of the state, and the relationships among economic, political, and social power.

Most controversial of all is the use made of Marxist ideas by Lenin and Stalin to create a form of dictatorship based in the Communist Party. Leon Trotsky (1879–1940), Lenin's ally and the rival of Stalin, argued that the revolution must be an active and ongoing process among the working class itself as it creates directly the forms of socialist life and work. Trotsky came to oppose the Stalinist position that the revolution must be primarily the work of the state and the party elite. Trotsky was assassinated by a Stalinist agent in 1940. His legacy of an antistatist version of Marxism lives on, particularly in the Third World, where Marx's nineteenth-century image of industrial capitalism never did have much relevance.[18]

Of a more conventional nature is contemporary "Eurocommunism." The communist parties of Western Europe have generally arrived at the position that the revolutionary overthrow of capitalism is not the appropriate method for achieving communism. Rather, they have adopted the path of participating in elections and working within parliaments and governments in the same fashion as other parties. Communism remains the objective, but the means of achieving it have shifted dramatically. While the power of nominally Marxist countries keeps the formal doctrine alive, currents of interpretation and revision of Marxist ideas promise new variations and experiments.

■ Postscript: Marx's Methodology

Another reason Marx is difficult to understand is that he uses a different method from what we are used to in explaining his ideas. The difference centers on his use of language. To put it in academic terms, Marx defines concepts by their relationship to each other, whereas we are used to conceptual definitions that tie each concept to some distinctive and specific meaning. For example, the concept of "class" might be defined by an income test: "lower class" could mean those making less than $10,000 a year, for example.[19] Marx defines "class" in relation to other concepts, such as alienation, exploitation, bourgeois-proletariat relations, or, indeed, its opposite, the classless society.

Class means one thing in nineteenth-century French society, with the remnants of a struggle among the feudal nobility, the rising bourgeoisie, and the developing urban proletariat. Class is something quite different in a modern industrial society. The difference lies, according to Marx, in the way that inequalities among people are generated by relationships based in different ways of producing goods and services. Because class is, in part, "defined" by its relation to changing modes of production, Marx's method allows him to capture the difference in a way that more conventional definitional techniques might miss. The problem for the reader of Marx is that definitions grow out of the relation of human development to historical circumstances, rather than being used consistently across time.

This method of definition offers considerable possibilities for exploring relationships in society. This is the method that allows Marx to see capitalism as a whole system of interrelated phenomena embracing everything from art to religion. Chains of interrelated concepts form the pathways through his system. The method also has the advantage of capturing the dynamism of history.

As Marxist scholar Bertell Ollman makes clear, all of Marx's key concepts are derived from his fundamental assumption about the human drive toward conscious production. A class-based society inhibits the fulfillment of our humanity; exploitation derives its evil character from the way that conscious productivity is denied to some for the profit of others, and so on. Marx's whole theory can be evaluated critically through the analysis of the validity of this fundamental assumption as it is worked out through his conceptual system. Upon this base depends his entire analysis of the meaning of alienation, the purpose of history, and the nature of politics.[20]

In another sense, the way that Marx's method is understood has a great deal to do with the kind of politics a Marxist would practice. In analyzing the uses of Marx's definitions, Terence Ball points out that if the world can be ordered in terms of precise concepts defined in positivist fashion by reference to physical sensations, then politics is nothing more than the implementation of a kind of mechanics of order.[21] If instead, as is true in Marx's thought, the world is seen to be changing in response to human design, then politics is about the realization of that meaning. The purpose of politics is both a process of discovery and an activity of directed energy.

Ball argues that Engels interpreted Marx's thought in a positivist fashion—one reason why Engels was so much appreciated by Western readers of Marx. He gave to Marx's ideas a (falsely) static set of definitions so that they could be understood in the familiar methodological style of a science. The danger was realized when Lenin and Stalin used this mechanical interpretation of Marx to create the Communist Party as an instrument for the uncompromising and insensitive administration of a theory of class conflict and revolution.

Marx, on the other hand, was the practitioner of a method that was historical in character, subtle and dynamic. As Ball points out, in Marx's conception, "The scientist never confronts nature, *simpliciter;* he confronts a humanly transformed nature and, as he confronts himself, a reciprocally transformed human."[22] There is nothing mechanical about his view of politics, or of the world. It is a place of struggle, of innovation, and above all change. That is what must be studied. A politics derived from that mode of understanding would be rather different from what is found today in most "communist" regimes.

■ Notes

[1] For a history of these notions, see Frank and Fritzie Manuel, *Utopian Thought in the Western World* (Cambridge, Mass.: Belknap Press, 1982). Cf. Christopher Hill, *The World Turned Upside Down: Radical Ideas During the English Revolution* (London: Penguin, 1972).

[2] Friedrich Engels remarked at Marx's funeral, "Just as Darwin discovered the law of development of organic nature, so Marx discovered the law of development of human history. . . ." "Speech at the Graveside of Karl Marx," in Robert Tucker, ed., *The Marx-Engels Reader*, 2nd ed. (New York: Norton, 1978), p. 681. This overstates the relationship—one that has an interesting history: see Terence Ball, "Marx and Darwin: A Reconsideration," *Political Theory* 7, no. 4 (1979):469–483.

[3] Here Marx differs from Darwin, who thought that evolution had no particular purpose other than facilitating survival. Marx believes that humanity has a destiny. Cf. Ball, op. cit., p. 473.

[4] Pierre Proudhon, a French utopian socialist theorist, is credited with the authorship of this phrase.

[5] For a selection of excerpts from Marx on life under communism, see David McLellan, *The Thought of Karl Marx* (New York: Harper & Row, 1971), pp. 212–224.

[6] On the relationship of Marxism to literary criticism, see Terry Eagleton, *Marxism and Literary Criticism* (Berkeley, Calif.: University of California Press, 1976), pp. vii, 15–17.

[7] Antonio Gramsci, the creator of the Italian Communist Party, develops the significance of political and cultural domination, or "hegemony," as the central aspect of class warfare. See Roger Simon, *Gramsci's Political Thought: An Introduction* (London: Lawrence and Wishart, 1982) for a useful guide to Gramsci's often confusing writings, specifically pp. 22–32.

[8] See Bertell Ollman, *Alienation: Marx's Conception of Man in Capitalist Society*, 2nd ed. (Cambridge: Cambridge University Press, 1976), pp. 193–194.

[9]Marx comments, "The aim [of the economists] is to present production . . . as encased in eternal natural laws independent of history, at which opportunity *bourgeois* relations [of production] are then quietly smuggled in as the inviolable natural laws on which society in the abstract is founded." Karl Marx, *Grundrisse*, Martin Nicolaus, trans. (New York: Vintage, 1973), p. 87.

[10]Karl Marx, *Grundrisse*, in Tucker, op. cit., p. 285.

[11]Cf. Friedrich Engels, *Socialism: Utopian and Scientific* (1892), in Tucker, op. cit., pp. 683–724.

[12]Marx, *Grundrisse*, in Tucker, op. cit., pp. 291–292.

[13]This was the view of Rosa Luxemburg (1870?–1919), the Polish Marxist revolutionary and critic of Lenin, Trotsky, and others. See Martin Carnoy, *The State and Political Theory* (Princeton, N.J.: Princeton University Press, 1984), pp. 61–65.

[14]See Alfred Meyer, *Leninism* (Cambridge, Mass.: Harvard University Press, 1957), especially p. 97 ff.

[15]See Leonard Schapiro, *The Origins of the Communist Autocracy* (Cambridge, Mass.: Harvard University Press, 1977). On Stalin, see Robert Tucker, "The Rise of Stalin's Personality Cult," *American Historical Review* 84 (1977):347–366.

[16]In Tucker, *The Marx-Engels Reader*, op. cit., p. 441.

[17]See Carnoy, op. cit.

[18]See Terence Ball and James Farr, eds., *After Marx* (Cambridge: Cambridge University Press, 1984), and Carnoy, op. cit., for a discussion of the varieties of Marxist thought.

[19]For a discussion of this method of definition, and the uses and limitations of the social scientific form of explanation that builds upon it, see Kenneth R. Hoover, *The Elements of Social Scientific Thinking*, 3rd ed. (New York: St. Martin's Press, 1984), pp. 3–46, 137–151. For a summary of the conventional critique of Marx's definition of class, see Peter Calvert, *The Concept of Class: An Historical Introduction* (London: Hutchinson Publishing Group, 1982).

[20]For further exploration of Marx's methodology, see Bertell Ollman, *Alienation: Marx's Theory of Human Nature*, 2nd ed. (New York: Cambridge University Press, 1976), and Paul Thomas, "Marx and Science," *Political Studies* 24, no. 1 (1978):1–23.

[21]Terence Ball, "Marxist Science and Positivist Politics," in Ball and Farr, op. cit., pp. 235–260.

[22]Ball, "Marx and Darwin," op. cit., p. 471.

SEVEN

Socialism in America must be seen as the deepening of democratic practices in the state, and the extension of democratic practices to the economy and family life. For socialism to come about, Americans must come to see it not as the excision of democracy from the state but its expansion in the state and its intrusion into the economy, where the despotism of the capitalist now reigns supreme, and into the family, where male supremacy and authoritarianism regulate the relations among men, women, and children.

Herbert Gintis (1983)

Socialism

Socialist ideas influence the public policy of every country in the world. From schools as public institutions, through legislation to protect workers and consumers from various abuses, to social security, socialist ideas are present in all but the most conservative party programs. Socialist parties provide the principal alternative to conservative rule in European countries. Variations on socialist regimes may be found throughout Africa and parts of the Middle East and in Central and South America. Canadian and U.S. politicians have adopted many ideas from the socialist tradition. If the Communist regimes of China and the U.S.S.R. be included, more than half the world's population lives in socialist countries.

All this has come about in the last century and a half, and much of it since the 1930s. As one historian remarked, "despite its failure everywhere to measure up to its original ideals, [socialism] has been one of the most successful political movements of all time."[1] What powerful vision lies behind this success? What ideas is socialism made of, and where did they come from? What are its strengths and weaknesses?

For many Americans, socialism appears as an idea that is vaguely understood and routinely dismissed as impractical. To many, socialism means governmental control of the economy, the loss of personal freedom, and economic inefficiency. There is some truth in all these generalizations, but they are parts of a stereotype that conceals more than it reveals about the socialist tradition—both its theoretical development and its impact on everyday life in the United States and throughout the world.

Our purpose will be to look for common themes in the variety of socialist visions rather than to represent the entire spectrum. Although there will be some general distinctions made among broad streams of socialist thought, we will be seeking a point of entry that will make the many versions of socialism more understandable. The description of the socialist vision will be synthesized from many sources, and the history of socialist experimentation will be presented as a way of illuminating the essential concepts.

Throughout this chapter, we will be exploring democratic and evolutionary approaches to socialism in contrast to Marx's conception of revolutionary socialism as a stage on the path to communism. The imagery of these two conceptions of socialism occasionally overlaps, but there are fundamental differences of both ends and means that distinguish them.

■ The Socialist Vision

Socialists start from the belief that human beings are social animals. A life dedicated only to the satisfaction of individual appetites is no life at all. The experience of working with others, living in a community of people with a shared sense of purpose, and making society responsive to the developmental needs of all its members is what makes for the fulfillment of human potential.

Socialists do not deny the significance of individual freedom. However, their conception of what it means and how it is attained is very different from that of liberals or conservatives. Individuality and sociality (to adapt a word) are not opposites; they are complementary. Only in a properly constituted society can people develop their individual talents and abilities. The quest for solidarity with others relies on human cooperation and is itself part of the maturation of the individual.

Socialists argue that the pressures of competition in capitalist society keep individuals divided on the basis of class, ethnicity, race, sex, and the struggle for survival. In a society based on cooperation, individual differences would be expressed as a matter of choice rather than of necessity. The main emphasis would be on mutual relationships of common work and shared expression "in which productive wealth is owned and controlled by the community and used for communal ends."[2] In socialist society, the individual would achieve freedom by participating as a mature citizen in a community of equals.

In capitalism, individuals can consume only what they are able to pay for, and the means of earning money are distributed very unequally. Through luck, class position, inheritance, or corruption, as well as hard work, some individuals gain an advantage over others. In the socialist ideal, goods and services would be distributed according to *need*. Need is defined generally as basic necessities plus whatever is required to support the individual's contribution to society.[3] In return, people would be asked to contribute to society on the basis of *ability*. In a secure environment with basic needs provided, individual talents could be cultivated without being held back by a class system or undermined by ruthless competition.

Although socialism would not abolish disagreements between people or resolve all differences among them, its advocates think that democratic methods offer the best chance of settling disputes and directing the uses of power to publicly beneficial ends. Instead of a few decision makers ruling by virtue of wealth, socialists foresee placing power in the hands of those most affected by the decisions and their consequences. By allowing people to share both participation and accountability, socialists expect that work would be performed more efficiently, productivity would be maximized, and the humane life would be possible.[4]

In Chapter Six we described Marx's communist utopia. Marx adapted the socialist ideal for his own purposes and emphasized its communal characteristic by calling the final stage of history *communism*. There is no need to repeat that description here. However, it is important both to see the differences between communist and democratic socialist ideas and to explore the contemporary issues raised in socialist thought.[5]

Marxism is frequently distinguished from socialism on at least two grounds. Many socialists do not believe that revolution is the proper means for transforming society, relying instead on the possibility of peaceful transition through democratic political institutions. Marx, on the other hand, thinks that socialism requires a revolution and must be enforced by the state as a means of achieving communism. Second, some socialists think Marx's vision of communism goes overboard in sharing too much of what must remain private if individual freedom is not to be lost to conformism and the terrors of the police state.

How Is Socialism to Be Achieved?

The differences over how to bring about socialism are profound. Contrast the following statements. The first is from the "Rules of the Fabian Society," an influential British democratic socialist organization. The second is from Marx's *Communist Manifesto*.

> The [Fabian] Society consists of Socialists. It therefore aims at the establishment of a society in which equality of opportunity will be secured and the economic power and privileges of individuals and classes abolished through the collective ownership and democratic control of the economic resources of the community. It seeks to secure these ends by the methods of political democracy.
>
> The Society, believing in equal citizenship in the fullest sense, is open to persons irrespective of sex, race or creed, who commit themselves to its aims and purposes and undertake to promote its work.[6] *(Fabian Society Rules, 1949)*

> The history of all hitherto existing society is the history of class struggles.
>
> Freeman and slave, patrician and plebeian, lord and serf, . . . in a word, oppressor and oppressed, stood in constant opposition to one another, carried

on an uninterrupted, now hidden, now open fight, a fight that each time ended, either in a revolutionary re-constitution of society at large, or in the common ruin of the contending classes . . . Our epoch . . . has simplified the class antagonisms. Society as a whole is more and more splitting up into two great hostile camps, into two great classes directly facing each other: Bourgeoisie and Proletariat. . . .

The Communists . . . openly declare that their ends can be attained only by the forcible overthrow of all existing social conditions. Let the ruling classes tremble at a Communistic revolution. The proletarians have nothing to lose but their chains. They have a world to win. WORKING MEN OF ALL COUNTRIES, UNITE![7]
(Communist Manifesto, 1948)

Notice that the Fabians appeal to all; Marx addresses the workers. The Fabians endorse equal opportunity; Marx advocates class rule. The Fabians propose to use the "methods of political democracy"; Marx incites revolution. Although there are common elements to their visions of the good society, the means of getting there are sharply different.

This difference in method led Friedrich Engels (1820–1895), Marx's collaborator, to label non-Marxist socialism as "utopian" socialism, whereas Marxism was to be seen as "scientific" socialism.[8] For Engels, the term *utopian* was one of mild contempt. He thought the images of utopia developed by Jean Jacques Rousseau (1712–1778) and the other intellectual patrons of the French Revolution had simply led to false movements toward reform. These movements, as in the case of parliamentary reforms, were taken over by the bourgeoisie as a way of pushing the old feudal nobility into the background. In his view the result of the French Revolution was the destruction of the feudal system and its replacement with rule by men of property.

Rousseau had a major influence on the style and development of socialist thought. He focused on the fundamental question: how to get people to look beyond their immediate self-interest to the larger interest of the whole community. Rousseau termed this larger interest the *general will*. People would be guided by the general will if certain conditions were met. There has to be a measure of equality so that "none would be so rich as to be able to buy another; and none so poor as to have to sell himself." Without such arrangements, the result is tyranny: the rich supply the financing for despotism, and the poor supply the tyrants themselves—an interesting prophecy of what happened in Germany in the 1930s. There need to be liberty of expression, active and effective participation of all citizens, and agreement that all laws will be made democratically and that the rule of law will be supreme. Under these conditions, individuals might become true citizens participating in the general will.[9] The French Revolution was filled with a Rousseauist rhetoric but lacking in any spirit of orderly process or common sense.

In the wake of the disappointments of the French Revolution, visionaries such as Henri de Saint Simon (1760–1825), Charles Fourier (1772–1837), and Robert Owen (1771–1858) constructed recipes for the establishment of ideal communities. Engels admired many of their ideas, but he scorned their simple faith that reason and idealism would somehow lead people to adopt these new forms. Marx's theorizing was different. By making the study of history into a science dealing with changing patterns in the organization of production, Marx had, Engels thought, given revolutionary communism an objective basis independent of any philosopher's vision of utopia.

History may judge differently which version of socialism was utopian. The ideas of modern democratic socialists owe much to these visionaries. Contemporary democratic socialist politicians have added to them a healthy respect for parliamentary democracy and the limits of the uses of authority in achieving change. The claim that Marxism is a scientific theory gave his revolutionary politics an absolute claim on people's loyalties—a claim that, in the hands of Lenin and Stalin, turned into a justification for a totalitarian system that resulted in the deaths of hundreds of thousands of people. The record of democratic socialist governments is far less bloody. The reforms they have achieved in education, health care, and worker participation in management, while not always successful, have by and large withstood the test of time and free elections.

Socialism and Personal Life

Socialists have classically argued for the extension of democracy from politics to economics—and also to social relations, including the family. What this means for parent-child relations and for sexual behavior has always been a source of controversy among socialists and a principal area of confrontation with conservatives.

Socialist criticism of the family begins from what is clearly a stereotype, though one that has much historical validity: the family unit as consisting of a father who holds a job and dominates the authority relations of the family; a mother whose work is confined to the home, who receives no wages, and who has minimal civil and political rights; and children who are subservient in every respect to their parents. Few families fit this description today, and for many families the stereotype always did overstate the reality of male domination.[10] However, the laws of Western societies have historically reinforced that pattern. It is these laws and

the conditioning to hierarchical authority in the family that socialists and other reformers have tried to change.

Socialists favor various kinds of "emancipation" from this version of the family with its male-supremacist, authoritarian characteristics. Seventy-five years ago, socialists in the United States
were struggling for voting rights for women, equal access to jobs,
and day care for children. Reforms of property law were to allow
women to own property in the same way as men and to have an
equal stake in the property acquired since marriage. The rights of
children were advanced through child labor laws and legal protection from parental abuse. Socialists are in the forefront of struggles for an expanded role for the community and the state in the
education and socialization of children.

Apart from these reformist measures, the principal improvement of family relations comes from the socialist principle of
substituting cooperation for competition in worklife. In a socialist
society, men would be released from the pressures of playing the
dominant role. Because people would be treated humanely in the
workplace, the connection would be broken that makes "macho"
behavior a compensation for powerlessness and exploitation on
the job. The humiliation that socialists see as the result of class
domination, competition, and alienation would be missing in
socialist society and the result would be healthier family relationships.

Some of the great socialist visionaries, including Marx at times,
advocated communal sexual and familial relations, an idea that
still remains controversial among socialists.[11] Marx thought that
the family was merely a disguised form of bourgeois rule over the
emotions, supported by property relations and surrounded with
hypocrisy. Adultery and the reduction of romantic feelings to property relations were what Marx saw in the family under capitalism.
Many socialists would agree with this critique, and add that the
family under capitalism is where children are socialized to a world
of inequality and domination. There is less agreement on what the
family should be and how politics is related to its development.
Although Marx at times advocated communalizing personal relations, the simple model of common kitchens, communal nurseries,
and free sexual relations has declined in popularity among socialists.

Socialists generally attempt to introduce elements of democracy
into personal life as a critique of relationships based on traditional
parental authority or economic dominance. Most socialists favor
community day-care centers, for example, not as a way of destroy-
ing the family but as a means of breaking the monopoly of male
power over the household. By this reform and others, a socialist

society attempts to supply the supports that increase the level of voluntary cooperation within the family. All socialists agree that the family will ultimately be a much healthier institution in a society that removes economic desperation, provides basic necessities, and encourages cooperation.

Contemporary American socialists are likely to view the family more with ambivalence than with distaste. It is seen as the place where a caring environment of mutual commitment can make life under capitalism "bearable." At the same time, under the pressures that capitalism creates, it can become a source of mental and physical oppression and of conditioning to a materialistic and competitive system. Given these polarities, some contemporary socialists favor the legitimation of many different living arrangements, from traditional heterosexual relationships, with or without legal sanction, to collectives for single people to gay/lesbian marriages. The determinant should be the needs of the individuals involved for personal growth and development, rather than legal restrictions or economic and social pressure. This alternative is recommended as both a release from the exploitative relations of capitalism and a realization of the freedom that a socialist society should allow in personal life.[12] The advocacy of diversity is part of an effort by socialists to build a coalition of groups that feel oppressed in modern capitalist society.

The controversies over how socialism is to be achieved and what it means for personal life are important in the history of socialism because they have often defined the limits of its appeal in democratic countries. At times, the liberalization of social mores has been a popular cause in the West, and socialism's support has helped to make it so. Women's suffrage was accomplished by building a coalition of socialists and many other reformist groups. In more conservative periods, socialism has been hampered by the reaction of moral traditionalists. The "New Right" in the United States has used traditional moral concerns as powerful issues against socialists, liberals, and the Left generally.

Similarly, the association of socialism with radical change, if not revolution, has tied the fortunes of the movement to changing tides of public satisfaction and discontent with the prevailing system. Socialism gained respectability in the United States in the twenties and thirties. A number of cities had socialist mayors; there were many socialist legislators. The Second World War and the reaction to the atrocities of the Stalin era discredited much of the Marxist and non-Marxist Left. Socialism became marginally respectable again only in the 1970s, following the development of the civil rights and antiwar movements and the Watergate scandals.

Although popular issues have affected the appeal of socialism, the heart of the ideology is in a vision of a more democratic relationship among the individual, worklife, and the state. Historically, realizing this vision has been the principal struggle. There is a great variety of recipes for achieving the socialist ideal, from small communes where everything is shared to planned societies where the principal industries are publicly owned and managed by the state. However, socialism has taken many forms, and we will summarize the development of the key ideas and experiments in the next section.

■ History of Socialist Experimentation

How would socialism work? Socialists share a common commitment to a distinctive mix of equality, democracy, and freedom, but the ideas that have shaped socialist thinking have emerged as much through practice as theory. This brief history will include an account of major socialist experiments as a frame of reference for the development of socialist ideology.

Socialist Prehistory: From Christian Communalism to the Rise of Cooperatives

Early Christian socialists believed that a simple life based on common work offered the best prospects for living the spiritual life. These believers took literally the biblical teachings concerning the equality of God's children and the preeminence of virtue over material gain.[13] Monastic communities are an expression of those ideals. Monks and nuns take the classic vow of poverty, chastity, and obedience designed to discipline the vices of greed, lust, and vanity. Communal living in a self-sufficient environment provided a separation from the sinfulness of the world and a means of reinforcing religious commitments that made the vow meaningful.[14]

These visions of combining spirituality with egalitarian forms of work and social life inspired seventeenth-century English rebels against the institution of private property. On the basis of religious inspiration, the "Levellers," led by Gerard Winstanley, aimed to "assemble a community, dig up and plant the commons, and live on their produce."[15] These movements were poorly conceived and badly led, but they gave fresh life to the ideal of spiritual reform through the organization of production on a cooperative basis.

As industrialization took hold of Western civilization, socialists focused on cooperative forms of factory production. Robert Owen, a Scottish industrialist, operated a large cotton mill in New

Lanark from 1800 to 1829 through methods that involved looking after the educational and social needs of workers and their families—and this arrangement became the basis for Owen's belief in cooperative communities with shared ownership of the means of production. Owen had many imitators. Although those communities ultimately failed for various reasons, they set a style for socialist thought. Variations have been tried many times since, and the notion of participative management has even found its way into the literature of contemporary business administration.

Owen also planted in socialist thought the idea that a person's character is the product of environment rather than of personal choice. If the environment could be changed to reinforce habits of cooperation and sharing, people would be less greedy and selfish. The vices attributed to capitalist competition and inequality would fade away. There would be no more vulgar displays of personal wealth. Poverty, theft, and prostitution would disappear. Owen's successful tenure at New Lanark demonstrated that such results were possible—at least in a paternalistic community that provided adequate services for its workers.

The argument that character is shaped by the economic environment separates socialists from Christian theology, with its emphasis on personal responsibility for sinful behavior. In many Catholic countries, an opposition was established in the villages between the priest and the schoolteacher, the former a conservative or at least a political skeptic, the latter a socialist and sometimes a Marxist. The essence of the argument was whether human nature was capable of improvement other than by personal self-discipline. The socialist contended that by changing the system of production, providing education, and breaking up concentrations of wealth, people's lives *and characters* would be improved. Socialism offered a path to the virtuous life separate from the path of religious commitment. In another sense, however, it allied socialists with various crusaders for moral reform.

In the past twenty years, the exchange between the Church and the Left has taken a new form. "Liberation theology," a radicalized version of the Christian message, has been formulated in Third World countries where the realities of exploitation are dramatically evident. In Latin America, people gather in "base communities," often with the guidance of clergy, to identify the sources of violence and misery that afflict their lives. By specifying the human dimensions of these problems, the people can take cooperative steps to solve them. This is a socialist approach to removing problems from the realm of destiny and fatalism so they can be addressed through collective action. Yet it builds on the inspiring example of Christ as an advocate for the poor.

A socialist initiative that seems to offer a successful model for modern economies is the experiment named after the community in which it began, Mondragon, in the Basque country of northern Spain. Mondragon is built around producers' cooperatives. Everyone who works in the cooperative contributes an initial share of money and participates in the direction of the enterprise through elected councils who hire managers. Originating as a worker-education movement in 1943, a small manufacturing operation was established in 1956. From there, the Mondragon "experiment" has grown to include more than 80 factories with 17,000 "cooperators."

In Mondragon, cooperatively organized banking and educational institutions were established and flourish to the point that they provide for the credit and training needs of the larger system.[16] The bank also lends money for initial shares to prospective workers. Mondragon has weathered rapid growth as well as economic stagnation without laying off workers or losing its momentum. Workers no longer needed in one industry are retrained through the educational system for other jobs. This example is now being carefully studied by socialists and others interested in a progressive form of productive community that is built from the ground up, rather than being implemented by the state.

Socialism and Economic Planning in Western Europe and the Third World

The cooperative movement is but one strand of socialist ideology; the growing power of the nation-state in the early part of the twentieth century placed the role of government at the center of socialist interest. Socialists advocated the democratization of political participation. They battled to extend the vote to women and minorities and to establish the presidential primary, among numerous measures. Along with successes in the movement to improve the access to power of millions of citizens came efforts to extend the reach of that power to more and more areas of community life. Socialist reformers concentrated on encouraging the extension of governmental responsibility for education, then the provision of basic utilities such as parks, electric power, and public transportation, and on toward the regulation and, in some cases, the public operation of basic economic institutions such as banks and communications systems.

The most characteristic expression of the statist approach to democratic socialism was the efforts in Britain and other European countries to combine parliamentary democracy with socialist economic institutions.[17] The First World War brought democratic socialists to power in Austria. The movement grew in other parts of the continent and it soon became an occasionally successful contender for power in Sweden and Britain. The early democratic socialist governments concentrated on improving services and setting the foundation of the modern welfare state. The Second World War brought new life to socialist ranks. The postwar socialist government in Britain nationalized the Bank of England, the railroads, and large elements of the coal and steel industries. The British Labour government also established a publicly financed health system with medical services and prescriptions available to all without charge.

In France, the government developed variations on planning involving private owners in semivoluntary arrangements with the government, the establishment of governmental planning agencies with considerable powers, and the extension of governmental responsibilities to a wide range of policy areas.[18] These innovations produced mixed systems in which the economics of the marketplace and the politics of democracy existed side by side in uneasy partnerships.

These arrangements occasionally were associated with reasonably successful strategies for economic modernization and growth, as in the Scandinavian countries, but also with big government and high taxes. The minimum socialist objective of providing for basic security was met through an extensive system for sustaining the disadvantaged. The larger goal of engaging people in a higher level of participation in the productive process remains more elusive. Nationalization of industries gave unions enormous power to strike against the government as a major employer, as in the coal mines or the railroads, and thus shut down the economy. This step led to wage rates that improved the lot of workers considerably, though sometimes at the expense of the position of an industry in international competition.

The power of capital was now confronted with the power of organized labor acting through socialist political parties. The confrontations over the last quarter of a century have generally been nonviolent, but bitter nevertheless. In Britain, the dream of a peaceful transition to a successful form of socialism was interrupted by the realities of economic decline as its empire was lost to independence movements in Africa and Asia. The rigors of increasing competition with low-wage Third World countries, and the burden on the social service system of increasing numbers of older citizens and children, are forcing Western European electorates to reevaluate the cost of providing high levels of publicly financed services.

Perhaps of longer-term significance than the cost problem, the cumbersome process of having politicians make economic decisions has had a decidedly mixed result. Socialist enterprises have had a hard time competing in a world economy where multinationals have the advantages of sophisticated marketing, political leverage, and mobile financial arrangements. Experiments with increasing participation on the part of workers have usually taken second place to the necessities of meeting the competition by using the techniques of centralized management. State socialism has sometimes merely added another remote and concentrated center of power, the bureaucracy, to the struggle for control. Critics on the Left began to point out that socialist political parties were losing their creativity and sense of vision. Governments became bogged down in making decisions among competing groups aiming for a larger share of the pie.

African experiences with socialism have encountered simultaneously the crosscurrents of tribal rivalries, the pressures of modernization, and the dangers of centralized state control. Many African leaders were deeply influenced by socialist ideas as they brought their countries to independence in the 1960s. Under their guidance, great gains were made in literacy, education, and public health. Yet they have not been able to translate European socialism into an African form that surmounts the problems of economic underdevelopment in the midst of global competition. Many avowedly socialist countries have had to turn toward attracting investments from multinational corporations as a matter of economic survival.

Socialist movements in Latin America have been strongly influenced by the forcible overthrow of the democratically elected socialist government in Chile in 1973. Chileans, angered by the redistributive policies of the socialist government, revolted with American help and a military dictatorship resulted. Democratic socialism as an alternative to the revolutionary model provided by Cuba has seemed an impossibility because of the military strength of the forces of capitalism. The Sandinista government in Nicaragua has followed a less repressive version of the Cuban model and is attempting to implement socialist educational and economic reforms in the midst of severe disruptions of its society from within and without. The problem of separating the Sandinista revolution from the Cold War context of superpower relations has not been overcome.

The twentieth century has provided ample proof that the advancement of socialist ideals by force is exceedingly risky. Yet the impulse to extend equality to wider spheres of life continues to take new forms as a political movement and, as the Mondragon example illustrates, through innovative experiments in the democratization of productive and communal life.

Socialism in Eastern Europe

Statism of another kind is evident in the socialist countries of the Eastern bloc, such as Poland, Hungary, Czechoslovakia, Roumania, and Yugoslavia. Here the introduction of socialism came from a combination of internal movements and Soviet political and military manipulation. The goal of socializing these societies by increasing the level of democratic participation has clearly been subservient to fitting the policies of each country to the requirements of Soviet control over foreign policy and economic development. Movements toward democratic reform were put down by military force in Hungary in 1956, Czechoslovakia in 1968, and, most recently, in Poland. These reform movements were nonetheless socialist and did not represent a movement to reinstitute capitalism.

Within these very severe constraints there has been some interesting experimentation with socialism. In reaction to the failures of the Stalinist model, efforts are under way to decentralize planning systems and increase the initiative of managers and workers at the plant level. In Yugoslavia, factories have been reorganized along the lines of producer cooperatives.[19] The attempt to form a free socialist union of workers in Poland achieved enormous successes before being put down by a Russian-backed takeover of the government by the Polish military. In Roumania, Hungary, and Czechoslovakia, factories and offices have been experimenting with previously unheard-of levels of autonomy from central control.

Eastern European socialism remains under the shadow of Soviet domination and of the system of rule by the Communist Party originated after the Russian Revolution. In practice, this relationship has meant that the party has a tight grip on all the major institutional positions of power—the media, universities, the military, factories, and others. Bureaucratization has a similar appearance in all statist societies. In the Soviet orbit, it is given a much more potent form due to the alliance between the governmental bureaucracy and the party.[20]

Where power is concentrated in this fashion, the temptation to corruption and arbitrary decision making is very great. The distinctions between party members and average citizens have led to feelings of resentment and alienation—most notably in Poland, where the system of giving party members preference for important jobs was one of the principal targets of the Solidarity protests.

Socialism in the United States

American socialism is in many respects more complex than European. Its sources are varied—from Christian and secular communitarianism practiced by early settlers to the dissenters against private property at the time of the drafting of the Constitution. Add to this mix successive waves of immigrants, among them all manner of socialists, reformers, and revolutionaries. The reasons for the weaknesses of socialist movements in the United States say as much as the successes about the meaning and relevance of socialist ideology.

The high point of electoral success for a party carrying the name *Socialist* came in the first two decades of the twentieth century. The United States at the turn of the century was the scene of massive labor struggles as the right to organize became established in a few basic industries.[21] The Socialist Party had more than 100,000 members and its candidate for president, Eugene Debs, twice received in the neighborhood of a million votes. There were fifty-six socialist mayors, including those in some of the largest cities in the country, and numerous socialist newspapers and local organizations.

The ideas in the platform of the Socialist Party were at times shared by populists and progressives and even elements of the Democratic and Republican parties. What was distinctive about socialists was their class-based approach to change. Progressives believed in strong government as an agent of reform, but they tried to appeal to all classes. Populists believed in the average citizen rather than elites, but not in the theory of the working class as the bearer of a special historical mission for the transformation of society. Socialists had their middle-class and even wealthy advocates, but their appeal was always to the special virtues and historical significance of the working class.[22]

Socialism is an ideology that sees the potential for a different world from the one we know. Building on the argument that social conditions shape human behavior, socialists believe that changes in those conditions will improve human behavior. For most socialists, the working class is the agent of change both because it is most directly involved with the key condition, the system of production, and because it is the direct victim of capitalist exploitation. The working class knows intuitively the meaning of work, the possibilities for the democratization of the workplace, and the necessity for change. The powerful figures of American socialism, Eugene Debs, Daniel DeLeon, and Bill Haywood, as well as intellectuals such as Max Eastman, understood and tried to work with this analysis.

Yet there were many obstacles to the development of class consciousness among American working people. Some derived from the special nature of American experience, others from the way that issues advanced by socialists divided working-class loyalties. No more diverse "working class" could be found on the face of the earth. Unlike the homogeneous European nations, the United States is an aggregation of immigrants from an array of ethnically and racially diverse peoples. There were even divisions within ethnic groups, such as between the first German wave, influenced by Marxist radicalism, and the second wave of German immigrants, inspired by Ferdinand LaSalle's democratic socialism. These differences complicated what was already an unlikely situation for the growth of militant class consciousness.

For class consciousness to develop, there needs to be a concentration of masses of people—yet, in the United States there was until the last few decades the frontier to absorb dissenters. The working class must also have movements to unite it around a clear ideologically based program. However, in the United States the labor movement was divided into many sectors, and the most powerful unions had a much simpler program: in the famous words of Samuel Gompers, a formative leader of the American Federation of Labor, "More!" The only major attempt at "One Big Union," The International Workers of the World under the leadership of Big Bill Haywood, fell prey to governmental repression, internal division, and a flirtation with violence that cost them their association with the Socialist Party.[23]

The notion of working-class solidarity had its internationalist dimension. On the American scene, internationalism undercut the socialists' ability to deal with the tides of popular opinion in two world wars. Eugene Debs opposed American entry into the First World War; he went to jail for arguing that it was a capitalists' war for which the proletariat provided the cannon fodder. The argument was popular among the believers, but the fight among the leadership and in the ranks over participation in the war sapped the Socialist Party and reversed its momentum. The "Red Scares" of the twenties added official repression to internal weakness, and "class consciousness" was weakened and dissipated.

With the consolidation of the Russian Revolution in the early 1920s, many American socialists found new hope. However, Lenin's path to change through the Communist Party was not based on any conception of democracy recognizable in the United States. As American leftists drifted toward the Communist Party, they became tied to Russia's foreign policy and to the Soviet model of centralized governmental planning directed by the party.

When the Depression seemed to fulfill Marx's prophecy of the collapse of capitalism, the Left became further entangled in the currents of Soviet politics. When Stalin made a temporary nonaggression agreement with Hitler, the notion of international working-class solidarity suffered a deadly blow. Although the Nazi invasion of Russia set the stage for a U.S.-Soviet alliance against Hitler, it did not restore the essential element of socialist politics: working-class solidarity. The American-Soviet alliance, which gave way soon after the Second World War to Cold War politics, was clearly based on national political interests, not the common struggle of working people.

An additional reason for the failure of class consciousness was the success of reformers who borrowed ideas from socialist ideology but left aside the rhetoric and the larger analysis of class conflict. From Roosevelt's New Deal to the Great Society programs of Lyndon Johnson, American politicians proved to be adept at using socialist ideas to contain grievances and rectify the most glaring effects of inequality. Their programs have often borrowed the ideas, but not the critique of capitalism, that socialists offer.

The only version of socialism that succeeded at all in the United States was based on democratic politics and a reformist program. It was called municipal socialism. The program concentrated on the efficient operation of public utilities and the expansion of public control to include transportation systems and small public housing projects. Coming to power in a number of U.S. cities in the twenties and thirties against a background of corruption and favoritism, the socialists emphasized clean government and democratic participation rather than class warfare.

Capitalism has not, on the whole, seemed exploitative to the working class. Rising prosperity has been attributed to capitalist efficiency and productivity, though it could be argued that it had something to do with massive governmental investments in the military, and the regulation of resource use and business practices by the government. However, this ability of capitalist political and economic systems to generate great wealth has disarmed class-based analysis and thereby deprived socialists of their basic tenet.

■ Conclusion

Socialists in the United States have never surmounted these obstacles. They remain active through such organizations as the Democratic Socialists of America, but they are effective only by communicating ideas that enter into the mainstream of party politics. The lack of a broadly based socialist movement makes the United

States distinctive among industrialized countries. It suggests that where class is less recognized or relevant, the socialists must pursue strategies other than emphasizing class conflict if they hope to expand their base.[24]

Meanwhile, reformist ideas have entered the mainstream of politics from other sources. Mass-based movements for change in civil rights, women's rights, and the environment prompted large-scale changes in rhetoric and policy. The countercultural movements of the 1960s and 1970s spawned many interesting conceptions of politics. The expansion of social scientific research in the areas of psychology and sociology opened up new ideas about human nature and its political possibilities. These initiatives are, in many cases, tied together by the theme of *liberation*—the subject of the next chapter.

■ *Notes*

[1]Albert Fried, ed., *Socialism in America: From the Shakers to the Third International—A Documentary History* (Garden City, N.Y.: Anchor, 1970), p. 1.

[2]Robert Kilroy-Silk, *Socialism since Marx* (New York: Taplinger, 1972), p. xv.

[3]For a thorough analysis of the concept of human need, see Patricia Springborn, *The Problem of Human Needs and the Critique of Civilization* (New York: Allen and Unwin, 1981).

[4]For a contemporary essay on socialist utopianism, see Michael Walzer, *Radical Principles: Reflections of an Unreconstructed Democrat* (New York: Basic Books, 1980), pp. 273–290.

[5]A critical perspective on socialism and the ideal of community is provided by Eugene Kamenka in *Community as a Social Ideal* (New York: St. Martin's Press, 1983), pp. 3–26.

[6]From the Rules as amended in 1949. In Anne Freemantle, *This Little Band of Prophets: The British Fabians* (New York: New American Books, 1959), Appendix B, p. 265.

[7]In Robert Tucker, ed., *The Marx-Engels Reader*, 2nd ed. (New York: Norton, 1978), pp. 473–474, 500.

[8]"Socialism: Utopian and Scientific," in Tucker, op. cit., pp. 683–717.

[9]See Sheldon Wolin, *Politics and Vision* (Boston: Little, Brown, 1960), pp. 370–71. Cf. Jacob Bronowski and Bruce Mazlish, *The Western Intellectual Tradition* (New York: Harper & Row, 1960), pp. 283–304.

[10]Less than one-fifth of the U.S. population lives in families that fit the pattern of a working father, nonworking spouse, and children.

[11]Lenin quickly disavowed this movement in Russia. To one socialist who claimed that sexual relations should be as free as drinking water, he responded that no one likes to drink from a dirty glass!

[12]See Lois Rita Helmbold and Amber Hollibaugh, "The Family in Socialist America," in Steve Rosskamm Shalom, *Socialist Visions* (Boston: South End Press, 1983), pp. 194–196, 216–222.

[13]Cf. Alexander Gray, *The Socialist Tradition: Moses to Lenin* (New York: Harper & Row, 1968) (1946), pp. 40–42 ff.

[14]See Albert Hirschman, *The Passions and the Interests: Political Arguments for*

Capitalism Before Its Triumph (Princeton, N.J.: Princeton University Press, 1977).

[15]Frank E. Manuel and Fritzie P. Manuel, *Utopian Thought in the Western World* (Cambridge, Mass.: Harvard University Press, 1979), p. 349. Cf. Christopher Hill, *The World Turned Upside Down: Radical Ideas during the English Revolution* (Middlesex, England: Penguin, 1972).

[16]See Henk Thomas and Chris Logan, *Mondragon: An Economic Analysis* (London: Allen and Unwin, 1982).

[17]A useful examination of the status of these experiments is found in Bogdan Denitch, ed., *Democratic Socialism: The Mass Left in Advanced Industrial Societies* (Totowa, N.J.: Allanheld, Osmun, 1981).

[18]For a survey of French socialism, see Stuart Williams, ed., *Socialism in France: From Jaures to Mitterand* (New York: St. Martin's Press, 1983).

[19]A probing study of socialism in the Yugoslav context is Svetozar Stojanovic's *In Search of Democracy in Socialism: History and Party Consciousness*, Gerson S. Sher, trans. (New York: Prometheus Books, 1981). The "official" Yugoslavian view of these experiments is presented in Edvard Kardelj, *Democracy and Socialism*, M. and B. Milosavljevic, trans. (London: The Summerfield Press, 1978).

[20]See Donald Hodges, *The Bureaucratization of Socialism* (Amherst, Mass.: University of Massachusetts Press, 1981).

[21]For an excellent review of this period, see John P. Diggins, *The American Left in the Twentieth Century* (New York: Harcourt Brace Jovanovich, 1973), pp. 60–63. Diggins reports that between 1881 and 1906, there were "some 30,000 strikes and lockouts, affecting almost 200,000 businesses and over 9.5 million workers" (p. 57).

[22]Aileen Kraditor, *The Radical Persuasion 1890–1917: Aspects of the Intellectual History and Historiography of Three American Radical Organizations* (Baton Rouge: Louisiana University Press, 1983).

[23]Diggins, op. cit., p. 60. Cf. David Milton, *The Politics of U.S. Labor* (New York: Monthly Review Press, 1982), for a sympathetic view of Depression-era labor radicalism.

[24]For an analysis of a contemporary American experiment in middle-class socialist politics, see Mark Kann, *Middle Class Radicalism in Santa Monica* (Philadelphia: Temple University Press, 1986).

EIGHT

The black ghettoes today . . . subsist on two kinds of economics: laissez-faire free enterprise capitalism, and welfare state, anti-poverty economics. Are either of these schools of economic method compatible with racial equality? They are not. Therefore logic demands that a movement for social change must be motivated by some other school of economic thought, or else it is fooling itself and wasting the people's time. This is especially true in view of the fact that both free-enterprise capitalism and welfare state economics are administered and controlled from the top down.

Harold Cruse,
*The Crisis of the Negro
Intellectual* (1967)

A person, after all, is not merely or exclusively (if at all) an objectified role-player or abstracted object of inexorable laws, but a thinking acting being engaged in particular relations with others within a specific historic time and place. To assimilate the public and the private into universal laws and abstracted structures requires Abstract Man, Abstract Woman, and Abstract Child in turn. Within this rarified, undifferentiated realm one searches in vain for a recognizable person and a redeemable politics.

Jean Bethke Elshtain
*Public Man, Private Woman:
Women in Social and Political Thought* (1981)

Liberation Ideologies

Liberation refers to freedom from some form of oppression. In the women's liberation movement, the objective is freedom from sexist discrimination. For those in the black liberation struggle, institutional and personal racism are the oppressors. The National Liberation Front (NLF) was the name of the coalition of forces in Vietnam that opposed the French and later the American role in Vietnamese affairs. As the opposite of oppression, liberation points to the removal of an abuse of people's rights, but there is not much content for a positive theory of what liberation really means.

What is liberation? Since the midsixties, the concept of liberation has taken on several meanings. It is becoming possible to construct from various examples and sources an ideology of liberation. Because this ideology has taken shape at least as much in practice as in theory, the construction is tentative, subject to several interpretations, and even contradictory. Although the movement has international dimensions, we will look only at developments in the United States, where some of the most advanced work in developing the practice and theory of liberation has taken place.

■ *A Vision of Liberation*

Defined negatively, liberation is freedom from any form of oppression. *Oppression* means the exercise of power so as to deny people a chance to live and express themselves as they wish. This concept points in the direction of a positive definition of liberation: it is the full realization of inner potential as an individual or a member of a community free of any constraining uses of power. As straightforward as that definition may seem, there is a tension in liberation ideology between its individualist and communitarian overtones, which will emerge as specific liberation movements are considered.

What would life be like in a fully liberated society? Essentially it would mean the acceptance of people on their own terms. Rather than having their existence defined and constrained by people of a different sex, nationality, race, or sexual preference, individuals would make life decisions autonomously or within communities of like-minded people. There would be no unequal treatment or discrimination arising from differences of gender, race, or sexual preference. Differentiation would be a matter of choice, not a policy imposed by a governmental or social structure.

Obviously there are conflicts among differing versions of a liberated existence. Emphasis in the Hispanic community upon the values of the traditional family might well conflict with feminist views on expanding the choices available to women. To resolve the conflicts on paper would be meaningless since they are very real in practice. What can be done is to assemble a composite view of liberation by identifying sources of oppression and examining what life would be like without those limitations.

The cardinal value of liberation ideology is equality. Equality is interpreted differently in liberation ideology from its meaning in socialism or classical liberalism. Socialists want to extend equality by democratizing the control of means of production; for classical liberals, equality centers on impartial treatment under the law. While liberation movements have included these approaches to equality, they have also added meanings having to do with practices of power that constrain people's prospects for advancement, undermine their sense of identity, and repress the expression of alternative cultural styles. Liberation ideology has broadened the meaning of "equal treatment" in confronting cultural practices and informal exercises of power that limit people's freedom.

Liberation movements have developed an understanding of power structures that go beyond governmental institutions. The experience of victimization at the hands of employers, social workers, and neighbors, for example, makes clear that the most telling forms of power are sometimes outside the government and beyond the reach of conventional politics.[1] Liberation movements have had to devise ways of confronting these inequities at their sources in social customs, habits, and informal structures of power. This wider conception of power and of politics is part of the value gained from studying liberation ideologies.

Women's Liberation

For the women's liberation movement, the principal sources of oppression are power structures based on presumptions of male superiority. In a world free of this oppression, women could, for example, compete for any occupation. Job discrimination based on differences in physical strength would give way to occupational reforms that would limit physical stress for both sexes. Job descriptions would serve the goal of sexual equality rather than of differentiation by sex. There would be no more "women's work" and "men's work." A redefinition of work so that either sex could handle any occupation would humanize work itself. Excessive lifting, unnecessary physical dangers, and hazardous environments would be eliminated for everyone.

Stereotypical characteristics such as differences in average physical strength and sense of compassion for others would no longer be used as arguments for sex-based occupational distinctions. Society would recognize that differences among individuals make averages meaningless as a basis for discrimination. There are strong women and weak men, compassionate men and dispassionate women.

For some women in the movement, the goal is a sexually neutral or unisexual society. For others, the goal is a society in which sexual differences are expressed only as individuals choose, rather than as a matter of enforcement by the rules of job, social life, and government. For the former, more radical group, child rearing would be oriented to eliminating sex-based distinctions. The daily tasks of caring for children would be split evenly and without regard for traditional role-differentiation. A conscious effort would be made to erase stereotypes of male-female behavior patterns that are embodied in laws and regulations.

Moderates in the movement would also deemphasize sex-based differences, but they do not insist that sexual neutrality is a goal in itself. Rather, they emphasize having the choice of crossing traditional lines without fear of criticism or social sanctions. The moderates concentrate on practical arrangements, often involving governmental policy, to increase the possibilities of choice: child-care arrangements to allow women to work, athletic programs for both sexes, paternity leaves from jobs as well as maternity leaves.

The moderates want to create a society in which sex-related traits can be expressed as freely as one can now express appreciation for music or a talent for mechanics. This vision does not rule out sex-based differences, but rather places them in a voluntary context within which they emerge by choice. Women should be as free as men to participate in sports, take stands on public issues, and be competitive or cooperative, as they wish.

The issue of abortion has been removed from a natural-law context and restated by the women's liberation movement as a fundamental issue of women's control over their own bodies. Again, the justification is phrased in terms of choice. Rather than having the government define the options for a pregnant woman, the women's liberation movement argues that it is basic to human freedom for women to decide that question for themselves.

The women's liberation movement has also worked toward overcoming indirect forms of discrimination. The issue of marital property rights involves the legal recognition of marriage as an economic partnership. By allowing property claims to be settled on the basis of who contributed income to the family, the law recognizes only the work of the partner who has a job outside the home. Work done within the home in raising a family is not accounted for. As a practical matter, this leaves women in a position of economic dependence upon men. Moving toward the concept of shared property rather than individual property grants both partners a claim on the resources accumulated in the course of a marriage.

The women's movement is not all pro-liberation. There is a powerful conservative women's movement that takes markedly contrasting positions.[2] Conservatives such as Phyllis Schlafly envision a world in which the law accords women a protected status that flows from their role as mothers of children. Occupational distinctions should be made based on strength, risk, and danger; for example, women would be excluded from the draft. The recognition of traditionally and religiously based rules for distinguishing between men and women would be allowed in the law. Abortion would not be permitted, for it is a violation of the right to life of the unborn. The traditional structure of the family would hold precedence in the law. Divorce would be difficult. Parents would have maximum leeway in governing the behavior of children. These positions contrast sharply with the liberationist vision because they start from the priority of traditional differentiations between the sexes.

The issues raised by women's liberationists reveal the way that sexual differences are often a central focus for organizing political power. Men occupy most major positions of power; sexual stereotypes are used every day to deny women equal treatment on the job; and property laws discriminate in favor of men in most states of the union. Such exercises of power are of course personal as well as governmental, but the women's liberation movement has used governmental action as a principal avenue in changing sex-related behavior. Affirmative action laws, marital property reform, and the legal controversy over abortion illustrate the point. In this respect, reform liberalism has been deeply influenced by liberation ideology (see Chapter Five).

It is characteristic of all the liberation movements that the identification of sources of oppression and of the political means for countering that oppression expands the meaning of liberation. Both the women's liberation movement and the long struggle of blacks for justice in the United States have illustrated the inseparability of the various dimensions of power—and the possibility of using one form of power to confront another.

Minority Liberation

Our planet is populated by minorities. For multi-ethnic nations such as the United States, the experience of minority status is part of most people's life history. Whether for Italians living in large cities, blacks in a suburb, or Hispanics in a rural area, the experience of minority life is quite diverse. At the same time, there are patterns that emerge. The patterns have surfaced in political writings that use the term *liberation* to deal with the issues facing oppressed minorities.

The use of the political process by minorities to remove barriers to freedom of choice form a continuing theme in American politics. In the nineteenth century, Northern European minorities such as the English, Germans, and Scandinavians, themselves often refugees from political and social oppression, came to North America and fought political battles to secure free public education, worker's compensation, and the regulation of industry and commerce in "the public interest." The public interest often had a decidedly ethnic twist to it, but it was the rationale for many expansions of governmental services designed to enhance the choices available at least to dominant ethnic groups.

Whatever the contributions of Western European ethnic groups to America's political history, the greatest sources of insight into liberation and oppression come from groups who were the most directly exploited: blacks, Native Americans, and Hispanics. The experience of each group has given a new meaning to liberation.

Slavery is the worst of all forms of oppression short of genocide.[3] The status of blacks as human beings was denied in the U.S. Constitution—blacks were treated in some provisions as property. The two-century struggle to escape slavery, and now racism and poverty, has given blacks in the United States a unique insight into the meaning of oppression. Native Americans were deprived of their homeland, though the reservation system provided a base for the continuation of Native American culture. Hispanics were also deprived, but they retained a cultural and territorial base in enclaves within the southwestern states. Blacks were enslaved, then freed formally but subjected to a system of legal oppression for more than a century while at the same time attempting to live as part of the larger society.

From the unique experience of blacks came a vision of liberation that was expressed first in religious terms and then in political movements. Black responses to oppression were based in the churches, in black schools, in the ghettos of large cities, and in the musical and artistic traditions of black culture.

In the powerful oratorical tradition of the black ministry, there is a vision of liberation as the abolition of racial barriers to individual freedom.[4] Martin Luther King, Jr. (1929–1968), was the leading modern figure of that tradition. He believed in the integration of blacks and whites on equal terms and in nonviolence as the means to change. Integration and nonviolence were linked in his mind.

King's nonviolent approach to change requires a faith in the ultimate decency of human beings; it is a sense of decency to which nonviolence appeals. He believed that there was more to politics than self-interest and the struggle for mastery. That same faith is required for races to learn to live together. It opens the door to reason, to compassion, and to a willingness to accommodate differences rather than insisting on conformity to a single view. King's vision of liberation provided not just aspirations but a method for achieving liberation. The nonviolent method itself contained the means for living in a liberated society.

Because Martin Luther King's message had a universal application to all sources of division in society, he could broaden his movement to include all the dispossessed and disadvantaged in society. He was developing a coalition of poor people across racial lines when he was assassinated.

In the ferment of the 1960s, other black leaders developed a set of ideas expressed in two slogans: "black is beautiful" and "black power." These slogans add an important meaning to liberation ideology by connecting politics to psychology.[5] Stereotypes and demeaning jokes are part of every minority experience. They are also part of the cultural uses of power to subordinate minority groups and women by enforcing a sense of inferiority in the consciousness of the oppressed. The "black is beautiful" slogan stood for an assertion that black culture and style have intrinsic values of their own. These values cannot be understood accurately, and should not be defined, by white cultural norms. The expression of this slogan in "Afro" hair styles, the study of black English, and the promotion of black studies are all efforts to reverse the disadvantages blacks suffer from the exercise of white cultural power.

Cultural power is not enough. The liberation of blacks in the United States required the deliberate exercise of black political and economic power. Some leaders felt that sharing power through alliances with nonblacks would always condemn blacks to a minor role. Independent black power was the condition of true advancement. Caucuses of black elected officials, the political organization of black neighborhoods, the development of black leadership, the organization of black economic enterprises, and even violence in the streets were all steps designed to make concrete progress toward ending the domination of the white power structure.

The linkage between cultural awareness, as reflected in "black is beautiful," and empowerment is a central characteristic of minority liberation movements. European ethnic groups in the United States developed positions of strength around ethnic societies, lodges, and neighborhoods and translated them into social status and political power. Although they were not labeled "liberation movements," the underlying realities were similar, if not as severe. In order to develop the self-confidence necessary to stand up to discrimination and to achieve liberation, a measure of pride is required.

The quest for liberation by women and minorities reveals many aspects of the linkage between psychology and power. The term that came to stand for this connection in the sixties was *consciousness*. Before women could advance the liberation movement, consciousness raising was necessary to make women aware of their condition and their potential. Consciousness raising is directed toward identifying sexist practices that are a nearly *un*conscious part of everyday life. The objective is to break down the assumption that sexism is a natural part of social structure. For blacks, the dominance of white economic and political power was an obvious fact of life. A precondition to confrontation, however, was a change in black cultural awareness and political self-confidence.

A similar pattern can be found in Hispanic and Native American liberation movements. In these cases, the historical basis for a distinctive culture is present, but the direct and indirect means by which the values of these cultures were undermined require careful consideration. By emphasizing the distinctiveness of their culture, Hispanics spoke out for a set of cultural values centered on the family and mutual assistance.[6] Native Americans stressed their cultural identification with nature and the concept of a living partnership between communities of people and their natural environment. Each of these movements confronted practices in white culture that degrade the family through excessive individualism and exploit the environment through pollution and the waste of natural resources.

Native Americans brought to liberation theory a sense of the significance of the environment as basic to human life. Many tribes had developed religious and mythological rituals expressive of that relationship. With an emphasis on tribal culture and environmental naturalism, Native Americans revived an understanding of the communal characteristics of human life and its dependence on a sensitive relationship with the natural environment.[7]

For Hispanics, family relationships are the crux of human development. They are the means by which life becomes whole. Without the family, people are reduced to individual striving and the limitations of personal ability. The natural emotions of affection, loyalty, and love are not developed in isolation. Hispanic writers have seen "Anglo" culture as hostile to the family because it stresses competition in an individualistic society. At the same time, Chicana feminists have been working toward redefining the patriarchal aspects of the family and the economy to allow for equity in the relation of men and women.[8]

Native American and Hispanic values stand in partial contrast to the notions of individual choice found in other versions of liberation. In traditional Native American culture, there can be no liberation of human beings as individuals acting only for themselves. The worst punishment a tribal society has to offer is banishment—being cast out of the tribe to confront life alone. Hispanics make a similar point with respect to the family and the consequences of its decline in contemporary society. The political expression of this viewpoint is found in the preference for communally based power structures wherein power flows from one's contribution to the group. Group solidarity has provided the basis wherever Hispanics and Native Americans have achieved a measure of political power.

Liberation: A Summary

At the beginning of this chapter, liberation was defined as "the full realization of inner potential as an individual or a member of a community free of any constraining uses of power." This definition is intended to point to a difference between individualist and communitarian understandings of liberation. There are conflicts between these versions. Women's liberationists have problems with family power relationships that favor males in Hispanic cultures, for example. At the same time the concept of solidarity in women's liberation reflects some of the same values of cooperative action with others in achieving a fuller life. These conflicts have not been resolved in theory or in practice. Liberation theory will be tested in the long term by its capacity to foster effective political action.

In the United States, liberation movements have in common a commitment to the use of governmental power to reverse cultural, economic, and psychological patterns of inequality. Government is perceived as an arena in which organized minorities can exert influence beyond their numbers through skillful coalition building, the consolidation of disciplined blocks of votes, and an appeal to the conscience of those in the majority. By these techniques, liberation strategists have made considerable advances for women and minorities by promoting presidential candidates, shaping legislation, and arguing cases before the courts. In other countries, where oppression is more directly evident, liberation ideology is associated with revolutionary action against conservative governments.

The key issues posed by the liberationist vision are two: the achievement of meaningful levels of choice for all individuals in the society and a consciousness of the role of solidarity, family, and community with others in human development. The first step for both the individualist and communitarian versions of liberation is the identification and elimination of sources of oppression. The second step is more complicated: the working through of a positive conception of liberation. In the conclusion to this chapter, and again in the final chapter, we will return to this theme to suggest some sources of understanding for the second step. For the moment, it is important to understand the outlines of the history that brought liberation ideology to its present state of development.

■ The Development of Liberation Ideology

There is a general pattern to the history of liberation movements in the American context. The crucial ideas, whether directed toward minorities' or women's status, show some interesting similarities. Equality has been the guiding value through a progression of steps beginning with arguments for civil rights, then cultural consciousness raising, then political and economic power.

These three phases overlap broadly and are different in each movement. Although a thematic history of the ideas is possible, it must be remembered that, in practice, each group has a spectrum of opinion. There are conservative as well as liberal blacks, moderate and radical Hispanics, and socialists as well as capitalists in all these movements. Here we are tracing the ideas of leaders and thinkers within each movement that have contributed to forging a new meaning for liberation. The ideas have influence well beyond their origins. They have contributed to the increasing power of the idea of liberation in American politics. Two of these movements illustrate the struggle most clearly: black liberation and women's liberation.

Black Liberation

The origins of black liberation are found in the experience of slavery. As slaves began with nothing they could call their own, not even legal recognition of their humanity, so the liberation movement had to be constructed from the ground up. The sources of the movement were in a remembered past of tribal life in Africa, the Christian message of salvation, and the painful struggle, sometimes in coalition with others, to meet the day-to-day challenges of advancing the cause of liberation.

Along the way, the writings, speeches, and sermons of black intellectuals contributed ideas and symbols that evoked powerful responses from racists, separatists, and integrationists alike. Separatism, as in the Back-to-Africa movement (1916–1923) under the leadership of Marcus Garvey, has always been part of the tradition. However, the leaders who shaped a new consciousness of black–white relations contributed the most effective elements of a theory of liberation.

In reaching to overcome barriers of racism, these thinkers were also showing people how to attack barriers to human development arising from class, ethnicity, and intimidation stemming from any source. Always at a disadvantage in terms of the ability to command force, the movement had to rely on persuasion, inspiration, and the creative mobilization of limited resources. The black liberation movement came to have a substantial relevance for all liberation struggles, whether by women, Chicanos, Native Americans, or, most recently, gays.[9]

The Christian religion contributed a mixed legacy to the black liberation movement. There was the powerful message of equality—that all people were beloved of God; that virtue and vice were distributed without regard to class, race, or status. The theme of deliverance from the toil and anguish of earthly life sustained many in their struggle for a better society, while it made passivity in the face of harsh treatment easier for others. Slaveowners, however, used biblical texts to justify mastery and encouraged Bible preachers to advocate obedience. Yet in the longer run, blacks were able to gain control of the uses of the Christian message and find in it, and in the structure of the church, the means to mount one of history's greatest movements of moral reform.

The political struggle to gain equality for blacks had its secular sources as well. Booker T. Washington (1856–1915) advocated self-help for blacks through technological institutes and other educational approaches. The National Association for the Advancement of Colored People (NAACP) was organized in 1910 and pursued antilynching campaigns, legal challenges to official discrimination, and the formation of a political coalition with moderate whites. The Congress of Racial Equality (CORE), founded by James Farmer in 1942, carried the struggle to the streets in nonviolent demonstrations that brought public attention to the injustice of discrimination. These efforts were built upon the unrealized promise of the Declaration of Independence, the Bill of Rights, and the Fourteenth and Fifteenth Amendments to the U.S. Constitution that all citizens are to be treated equally under the law.

Martin Luther King added to the inspiration of the Gospel what Christianity lacked in political terms: a technique for translating faith into political action. King studied the techniques of nonviolent direct action developed over the decades of India's struggle for independence from Great Britain. Mahatma Gandhi was King's political inspiration. Under Martin Luther King's leadership, thousands of blacks and their allies used nonviolent tactics to display for all to see the cruelty, bigotry, and violence inherent in racism. They forced the desegregation of accommodations and public facilities in hundreds of communities. The combination of these elements into a single activist faith was immensely powerful. King brought it together in Washington, D.C., on August 28, 1963, in his famous "I Have a Dream" oration:

> With this faith we will be able to work together, pray together, struggle together, go to jail together, stand up for freedom together, knowing that we will be free one day. . . . When we let freedom ring, when we let it ring from every village and every hamlet, from every state and every city, we will be able to speed up that day when all of God's children, black men and white men, Jews and Gentiles, Protestants and Catholics, will be able to join hands and sing in the words of the old Negro spiritual, "Free at last! Free at last! Thank God Almighty, we are free at last!"

Separatism and Radicalism

Yet there were doubts within the movement about the effectiveness of nonviolence. Malcolm X, in his early phase as a radical leader of the militant Black Muslims, pointed out: "There is a big difference in the passiveness of King and the passiveness of Gandhi. Gandhi was a big dark elephant sitting on a little white mouse. King is a little black mouse sitting on top of a big white elephant."[10] A cadre of younger black leaders began to break with King on the direction of the movement: the Student Nonviolent Coordinating Committee (SNCC) became more militant under the leadership of Stokely Carmichael; the Black Panthers implemented separatist black movements in Oakland with Huey Newton and in Chicago with Fred Hampton. The threat of violence was brought forward as a tool to move the white establishment.

The militant separatist analysis led in a different direction from King's integrationist vision. For some black leaders, separatism, like violence, was a tactical issue, and there were splits over the use of coalitions with whites in the struggle for racial justice. The question was whether a reliance on white participation weakened the resolve of the movement and undermined the claim of blacks to be able to control their own destiny. Few black leaders saw separatism as a complete solution to white oppression, though even King was aware that a measure of self-conscious pride was a vital ingredient in advancing the cause.

The shift from the use of the term *Negro* to the term *black* was intended to direct attention away from racial characterization and toward a distinction based on power. Stokely Carmichael and Charles Hamilton were among those who argued that whites were identified not by racial characteristics but by color. Color was used as a basis for an exercise of power disadvantageous to blacks. Referring to "blacks" rather than to "Negroes" drew attention not to race but to power, which was at the root of the problem.[11] In this way, a bridge was constructed from the phase of consciousness building to the active pursuit of power. Stokely Carmichael brings together the movement toward black consciousness and the cry for black power:

> The word love is suspect; black expectations of what it might produce have been betrayed too often. But those were expectations of a response from the white community, which failed us. The love we seek to encourage is within the black community, the only American community where men call each other "brother" when they meet. We can build a community of love only where we have the ability and power to do so: among blacks.[12]

The move to emphasize the distinctiveness of the black experience and identity led to experimentation and conflict within the black community. For Stokely Carmichael, the trail led to the advocacy of new versions of Marxism developed in Africa and the Caribbean. In the tradition of W. E. B. DuBois (1868–1963), who combined the politics of racial separatism with Marxist class analysis, Carmichael became a radical force in the black liberation movement.[13] Yet Carmichael, unlike Huey Newton and other Black Panther leaders, insisted that race is more important than class in the structure of oppression.

There were more moderate versions of the black power movement. For Charles Hamilton, the emphasis on black independence and the development of effective bases of power led toward electoral mobilization as the key to liberation. Hamilton also advanced projects designed to replace the welfare system with cooperatives for housing and other purposes. By using benefits from the welfare system plus personal labor, urban blacks could develop a modest investment stake that would permit partnerships in the renovation of homes and the development of small businesses.

For Martin Luther King, the logic of the movement led in another direction than separatism. King maintained a dialogue with separatists on the tactical aspects of the issue and gave ground very grudgingly. At the same time, he began to broaden the liberation struggle: King made common cause with poor whites in an antipoverty crusade and with the antiwar movement in opposition to the war in Indochina. To those who characterized his movement as passive, he rejoined that the meaning of Gandhi's technique was anything but passive—it was the active confrontation of evil with the power of love expressed in militant nonviolence.

The white violence that came in response to black nonviolence escalated during the sixties. In SNCC's "Freedom Summer" of 1965, six were killed, eighty beaten, more than a thousand arrested, and sixty-eight churches and homes dynamited.[14] Yet the movement scored its greatest triumph in that year with the passage of the Voting Rights Act of 1965, which led to the effective enfranchisement of millions of blacks and the widespread passage of open housing laws. The culmination of the cycle was the assassination of King in Memphis in 1968. There were rebellions, riots, and uprisings in fifty-seven cities in the United States that summer.

As the movement struggled on through the seventies, it kept its roots in religion. The churches provided the sanctuaries, the spiritual sustenance, and the leadership training for generations of black activists. The religious dimension of the black power movement is also expressed in Muslim churches. In the theology of some Muslim sects, it is black people rather than Jews who are identified as the "chosen people" of the Old Testament.[15] For other Muslim leaders, Islam offers a unifying faith that can bring oppressed whites and blacks together in a common struggle for justice.[16]

Religious differences have important impacts on the political strategies pursued by activists in the black community. One strategy, separatism, points toward the selective mobilization of black loyalists; the other strategy leads toward coalitions with other oppressed people. Political leaders such as the Rev. Jesse Jackson can use both strategies, mobilization as well as coalition, to forge a broadly based "Rainbow Coalition" of the poor, the elderly, women, and other groups that have felt excluded from structures of power.

The Limits of Protest

With the reverses in the economy after the Arab oil crisis in the late seventies and the deindustrialization of the job structure, the black liberation movement became less visible. The struggle to maintain jobs and governmental benefits in a sector of the economy in which opportunity was rapidly diminishing divided blacks and their white liberal allies. Affirmative action programs became steadily more controversial. The dominant perception changed from a sense that the poor are the victims of exploitation to the idea that they are the beneficiaries of a corrupt and economically inefficient welfare system. These changes of perception, regardless of the evidence on the efficacy of governmental antipoverty programs, along with division in the ranks of black leadership, badly weakened the movement.[17]

Like women's liberation, the black liberation movement began to lose momentum when it moved from cultural and political issues to the divisive problems of economic gains and losses. Civil rights and cultural recognition do not put bread on the table. Overcoming discrimination in hiring practices ultimately comes down to establishing quotas, setting aside normal channels of promotion, and attacking union seniority rules. Going beyond a piecemeal approach to these barriers meant taking on the whole issue of the fairness of capitalism—and the consideration of socialist alternatives.[18]

Under these conditions, it became increasingly difficult to maintain the commitments from allies in the unions and among urban liberals that helped clear the path for reform. The victories of a conservative administration in 1980 and 1984, partly in reaction to these pressures, gave prominence to the arguments of Thomas Sowell, a conservative black intellectual who maintains that governmental programs and economic regulation do more to hinder black progress than to help it.[19]

What remains in the 1980s is a sense that something was said in the sixties about the meaning of human liberation, that important gains were made, but that the movement ran into major obstacles in a time of economic change and disruption. For Jesse Jackson, who in 1984 became the first American black ever to mount a credible national presidential campaign, the task was to interpret the needs of the downtrodden to an electorate wary of programs and preoccupied with its own economic position. Progress was made against overt personal and legal discrimination, but the struggle against institutionalized racism is much larger and even more complex. At the same time, blacks have gained positions in the cultural and political power structure of American society and have begun to establish a base in major cities and in the Congress for a new formulation of the liberation movement. The problem of defining a new vision of liberation remains—and we will return to it in the conclusion of this chapter.

Women's Liberation and Feminism

The feminist movement has a long history in the United States. There was serious agitation for women's property rights in the middle of the nineteenth century. The latter part of the century saw the rise to prominence of the suffragist movement, and with the constitutional amendment to extend to women the right to vote in 1915, a major objective was accomplished. Feminism then entered a new phase—seeking a program and an ideological orientation that would address the more comprehensive questions of women's role in social, political and economic life. That phase came to fruition after the Second World War as feminist writers began exploring the themes that are common to liberation ideology.

There were three basic viewpoints that served as beginning positions for the development of women's liberation ideology: conceptions of inherent differences between the sexes, theories based on liberal individualism, and socialist analyses of the relationships among class, sex, and power. These viewpoints, brought together in various combinations, provided an abundant source of insights about the uses of power in oppressing and liberating women.

The Political Uses of Sexual Differences

The argument that there are inherent differences between men and women is indisputable on one level: biology. The question is how that should affect the relationship of men and women to political power. Both feminists and defenders of traditional sex roles have argued, for quite opposite purposes, that the differences are crucial.

The argument that women are destined by biology to functions based in the home was the justification for exclusively male suffrage and male property rights. Marital arrangements that gave to men the preferred legal status were a reflection of the presumed superiority of the male role in the productive as well as the public sphere. It was the perception of this arrangement as oppressive that generated the modern feminist movement.

There is a long tradition of feminist writers who argue that there are indeed inherent differences and that women are superior in qualities important to political life. Elizabeth Cady Stanton (1815–1902), at the end of the nineteenth century, pushed for female suffrage on the grounds that women would bring idealism, virtue, and morality to politics. If women were involved in politics, they would redeem the male qualities of self-serving, violent, and acquisitive behavior.

A subtler point of view was expressed by the existentialist philosopher Simone de Beauvoir in *The Second Sex*, published just after the Second World War. She maintains that women are indeed inherently different, and acknowledges that their special relationship to childbearing places them at a disadvantage in the world of power and politics. To enter the public world, it is necessary to transcend private concerns; so women must strive to overcome the limitations of domesticity that nature places upon them. Her early version of consciousness raising had to do with encouraging women to aspire to the role that men play by rising above their historical limitations. She advocates equality, but the meeting ground is in a man's world of power, responsibility, and self-assertion. She calls upon men to assist in this task:

> It is for man to establish the reign of liberty in the midst of the world of the given. To gain the supreme victory, it is necessary, for one thing, that by and through their natural differentiation men and women unequivocally affirm their brotherhood.[20]

She foresees a world of social and political equality based on a mutual acknowledgment of differences. Customary practices that condition men and women to relations of inferiority-superiority can be overcome by a new generation that is willing to struggle for equality.

The search for an authentically feminist position on life and politics is one that can lead either toward integration in a sexually neutral society or toward separatism in the name of female autonomy. Feminists are divided over the usefulness of emphasizing the uniqueness of women's role and identity in history and myth. Some see that emphasis as a prerequisite to self-respect and others as a trip into nostalgia that takes away from more practical struggles.[21]

More militant contemporary feminists have used sexual differences to advance the position of separatism. Ti-Grace Atkinson, Susan Brownmiller, and Mary Daly have all argued that the male capacity for sexual aggression is carried into other spheres of life. Contemporary politics, religion, and cultural practices are, like sexual relationships, basically oriented to the exercise of male domination over women. For these women, the solution lies in consciousness of a different sort. Women must organize to protect themselves and create a separate existence removed from male aggrandizement. The furthest extension of this position is the advocacy of lesbianism as a solution to male aggression and domination.

Liberal Feminism

Liberation movements draw much of their imagery of individual freedom from classical liberal political thought. The classical liberal tradition never depended on the notion that all people are the *same*, but rather, asserted that all individuals are entitled to equal treatment under the law. Liberal feminists have used the language of reform liberalism to argue for equal rights to the vote, to the ownership of property, and to employment opportunity. The main initiative has been the Equal Rights Amendment to the U.S. Constitution.[22]

The concept of affirmative action takes the next step beyond equal treatment under the law: government enforces positive action rather than merely assuring a fair process. Affirmative action policies require that government help overcome previous discrimination by assuring that women (and minorities) be given particular consideration in awarding financial aid, or hiring, or other actions affecting opportunities for advancement. This policy puts the burden on employers to prove that they have actively sought out women and minority candidates. It has led, in some instances, to modified quota systems by which a court, for example, will require that a fire department hire no more men until it has hired a certain percentage of women.

A step further is the movement for "comparable worth" as a principle in determining levels of pay. The movement comes from the perception that women are confined to a very few occupations by a history of discrimination against women in educational, social, and psychological respects. The result has been that these occupations are poorly paid regardless of the level of responsibility and skill involved. A secretary who has to make a variety of independent judgments, deal with the public, and use several kinds of office machinery is paid at a lower rate than an assembly line worker who has less responsibility and requires less training. The proposal is to legislate the requirement that jobs of *comparable* difficulty and responsibility be compensated at the same rate. The result is the removal of sex as a factor in determining pay. The movement not only extends the argument of equal treatment under the law but moves it into the economic sphere.

The liberal argument does not attempt to resolve the question of sexual differences. In liberalism, all individuals are perceived as unique and distinctive. The state is based not so much on an image of a uniform human nature as on the need to have a rational basis for resolving conflicts between individuals. By implementing equal opportunity policies, affirmative action programs, the drive for the Equal Rights Amendment, and now comparable worth, reform liberal feminists have given the liberation movement a specific political program.[23]

The theoretical advance involved in liberal feminism is in the work done on environmental conditioning as a factor in sexist discrimination. The argument is that sexual differences are largely socially induced. Girls are taught to like dolls, whereas boys have toy guns. Altering conditioning through consciousness raising as well as changes in the law can change the pattern of social conditioning. For this reason, it is important to make sports programs available to women and nursing careers to men, for example. Since schools and other public agencies play a large role in socialization, governmental action can be taken to attack the pattern of sex-related socialization. Such action is justified in the liberal frame of reference as a way of moving toward the nondiscriminatory uses of public power on behalf of all citizens.[24]

Patterns of socialization are the most complex aspect of society. They touch on the most intimate details of customary practice and private relations. By bringing these patterns into the public arena and making them an explicit target of reform, liberal feminists have stirred up enormous opposition from traditionalists and conservatives—both male and female. Yet these patterns are the basis for the daily exercises of power that shape people's lives.

One question that any political ideology must answer is the extent and direction of change in the patterns of socialization that can be accomplished by political action. Those who believe strongly in the power of environmental conditioning see these patterns as flexible; conservatives see them as fixed in human nature. We will have more to say about this below, but first it is important to consider the perspectives of socialist feminists.

Socialist Feminism

Socialist feminists point out that neither the feminist separatists nor the liberals deal with the problem of class and its impact on women. Taking some of their text from Marx and Engels' analysis of capitalism, socialist feminists see their oppression as being intimately tied to capitalist exploitation. Simply to enable women to compete in the marketplace on the same terms as men is only to subject them to the same forms of specialization, alienation, and exploitation that men experience. There are several variations on this position, and they reveal interesting sides of the problem of developing an ideology of liberation.

Marx thought that the oppression of women under capitalism was centered in the use of the family system as a way of getting women to do the socially necessary task of bearing and raising children with the least possible compensation (see Chapters Six and Seven).[25] All sorts of barriers to the entry of women into commodity production, from lack of educational opportunity to outright legal discrimination, constrain women to remain in the home without an independent income. Marriage under these circumstances becomes a relationship of economic domination. Friedrich Engels envisioned that communism will, by providing for the basic needs of all, remove economic necessity as a factor in marriage and allow family relationships to develop on a basis of love and mutual commitment.[26]

The basic theme of socialist feminists is that capitalism stands in the way of liberation for women. Angela Davis suggests that capitalism, by creating an economy outside the home, led to the downfall of the women's vital role in production. The market economy devalued the home economy, the province of women, and left them in a dependent status.[27] The solution is a form of socialism under which community-owned production will involve the concept of day care and the reconceptualization of housework as a part of production to be shared by all.

Some feminist theorists have taken the argument an important step further. They have argued that sexism precedes capitalism and that patriarchy and capitalism are co-conspirators in the oppression of women.[28] At the same time, sexism is not automatically solved by socialism. The problem is to go beyond Marx and Engels and create the structure of power that would permit a community to be free of both class-based and sex-based oppression. This is the frontier of liberation theory.

■ Conclusion: What Is Liberation?

These currents of thought and the political movements that have expressed them have generated new insights into the meaning of human liberation. The clarity and consistency of classical liberal ideology has not yet been achieved, but there are the elements of a new ideology that can be drawn from these ideas.

Liberation ideology struggles for definition in the contested terrain between liberal individualism, conservative institutionalism, and Marxist communitarianism. Throughout most of these writings there is the sense that people are individuals who deserve to be free of domination in the name of sex, race, or class. At the same time, there are suggestions that the meaning of liberation is more complicated than simply being free to do whatever one wishes. The idea that a fully human person is one who is at home in various institutional and communitarian arrangements having to do with personal, political, and productive life is found throughout the literature of liberation. Similarly, there is a pattern in the identification of the institutional and structural forms of discrimination that underlie individual attitudes.

For contemporary theorist Jean Bethke Elshtain, the problem of liberation has to do with constructing an understanding of the relationship between the private and public realms of life.[29] She does not find liberation in an ideology that abolishes the personal sphere by picturing life as entirely bound up with questions of race, class, and sex. On the other hand, the notion that we can be autonomous individuals flies in the face of the human condition. We are the creatures of family, shared language, and community. We are not simply class clones, the products of a socially determined role structure, or, for that matter, free agents inventing our own lives in isolation from others. Class structures and role models are highly significant, but there are other forces at work: self-reflection, instinctual urges, emotional ties to others, and the variations that time brings to life.

Liberation, in this view, becomes the capacity to find a sense of roots in personal life that allows significant participation in a public life open to the possibility of change and growth. The private sphere, as Elshtain describes it, must be "a locus of human activity, moral reflection, social and historical relations, the creation of meaning, and the construction of identity having its own integrity."[30] The private life is where liberation comes home to a humane personal existence. The family is the critical institution in which the private and public realms meet.[31] The public realm will not contain all the answers to human problems. But the public realm must center on a process by which limits on private action can be defined in an atmosphere of inquiry, flexibility, and humanitarian concern. What destroys the public realm is totalistic ideologies that define away private life and individuality in the name of salvation and certainty, or the possibility of community in the name of unfettered individual freedom.

Part of what Elshtain speaks of was learned in other ways by minorities in their struggle for liberation. What blacks in centuries of struggle against racism learned about the need for roots in a community of religion, Native Americans learned in relation to the tribe, and Chicanos in the family-based community. The message of liberation ideology is that these insights must be applied somehow to public life. The human personality requires nurture, shared meanings, and a measure of structure in order to develop. There must be the room, the freedom, for these relationships to be created by individuals who can explore and choose and make commitments.

Martin Luther King, in his philosophy of "personalism," asserts that human beings must retain the initiative in the battle against personal and social evil.[32] Militant nonviolence is the form of collective action that brings the individual into association with others in an arena where evil can be exposed and truth can be discovered through joint action.

In this vision of liberation, there is no conclusion to the business of the public realm; the community must be made and remade by each generation as individuals work through the development of personal identity in a humane environment. Erik Erikson, the principal theorist of the formation of human identity, points out that all human beings seem to strive toward a sense of *competence* and *integrity*. By competence Erikson means the capacity to perform tasks of personal development and economic production in a manner that is qualitatively pleasing. At the same time, people aspire to a sense of integrity, or wholeness, by which the pieces of life come together with a meaning and purpose that generates a satisfying self-concept. When these drives are frustrated or diverted by environments and forces that exploit, oppress, and corrupt, they are perverted into pseudo-identities based on racism, sexism, and the pathologies of personal and social destruction.[33]

In the end, the tension that exists in liberation thought between individualist and communitarian emphases can be resolved only by a careful consideration of the boundary between public and private life. There can be no private liberation in a hostile public environment; and the liberation of one community cannot come at the expense of legitimate individual rights for all. By probing some of the frontiers of this question and its relationships to the psychological and cultural dimensions of power, liberation ideology has contributed important new insights to political understanding.

■ Notes

[1]For an examination of these informal sources of power, see Murray Edelman, *Political Languages: Words That Succeed and Policies That Fail* (Madison, Wisconsin: Institute for Research on Poverty Monograph, 1977).

[2]For comparisons of feminist and conservative approaches to abortion and other issues, see Pamela Johnston Conover and Virginia Gray, *Feminism and the New Right: Conflict over the American Family* (New York: Praeger, 1983), and Marilyn Falik, *Ideology and Abortion Policy Politics* (New York: Praeger, 1983).

[3]A classic first-hand account of slavery is Frederick Douglass's *Narrative of the Life of Frederick Douglass, an American Slave* (Garden City, N.Y.: Anchor Doubleday, 1845, 1973).

[4]See Charles Hamilton, *Black Preacher in America* (New York: Morrow, 1972).

[5]On the psychological aspects of racism, see William Grier and Price Cobbs, *Black Rage* (New York: Bantam, 1968). A unique perspective on racism is provided by

white author John Howard Griffin in *Black Like Me*, 2nd ed. (New York: Houghton Mifflin, 1977)—the story of his travels while disguised as a black.

[6]See Armando Rendon, *Chicano Manifesto* (New York: Macmillan, 1971); F. Chris Garcia, ed., *La Causa Politica: A Chicano Politics Reader* (Notre Dame: University of Notre Dame Press, 1974).

[7]Alvin Josephy, *Now That the Buffalo's Gone: A Study of Today's American Indians* (New York: Knopf, 1982).

[8]See Alfredo Mirande and Evangelina Enriquez, eds., *La Chicana: The Mexican-American Woman* (Chicago: University of Chicago Press, 1979).

[9]See John D'Emilio, *Sexual Politics, Sexual Communities: The Making of a Homosexual Minority in the United States* (Chicago: University of Chicago Press, 1983).

[10]Stephen Oates, *Let the Trumpet Sound: The Life of Martin Luther King, Jr.*, p. 244.

[11]Stokely Carmichael and Charles Hamilton, *Black Power: The Politics of Liberation in America* (New York: Vintage, 1967). Cf. Floyd Barbour, ed., *The Black Power Revolt* (New York: Collier, 1968).

[12]In Barbour, op. cit., p. 75.

[13]For an exploration of the relationship of black liberation and Marxism, see Cedric Robinson, *Black Marxism: The Making of the Black Radical Tradition* (London: Zed Press, 1983).

[14]Oates, op. cit., pp. 300–301.

[15]See Charles E. Lincoln, *The Black Muslims in America* (New York: Greenwood Press, 1982).

[16]Malcolm X came to this view after a visit to Mecca. See *The Autobiography of Malcolm X* (New York: Ballantine, 1977).

[17]For additional analysis of the splits within the movement, see Peter Goldman, *Report from Black America* (New York: Touchstone Books, 1971), Chap. 2.

[18]This realization is detailed in Robert Allen, *Black Awakening in Capitalist America* (New York: Doubleday Anchor, 1970).

[19]*Markets and Minorities* (New York: Basic Books, 1981); *The Economics and Politics of Race* (New York: Morrow, 1983).

[20]Simone de Beauvoir, *The Second Sex* (New York: Vintage, 1945, 1974), p. 689.

[21]To explore the two sides of this debate, see Nina Auerbach, *Women and the Demon: The Life of a Victorian Myth* (Cambridge, Mass.: Harvard University Press, 1982); Annis Pratt, *Archetypal Patterns in Women's Fiction* (Bloomington: Indiana University Press, 1982); Barbara Rigney, *Lilith's Daughters: Women and Religion in Contemporary Fiction* (Madison: University of Wisconsin Press, 1982). Cf. Heather McClave, "Scholarship and the Humanities," in Barbara Haber, ed. *The Women's Annual 1982–1983* (Boston: G. K. Hall, 1983), pp. 205–229.

[22]Though this has been the work of large organizations such as the National Organization of Women rather than individuals, Betty Friedan provided substantial intellectual and political leadership through her *The Feminine Mystique*, 20th anniversary ed. (New York: Dell, 1984) and *The Second Stage* (New York: Summit Books, 1982).

[23]See Kirsten Amundsen, *The Silenced Majority* (Englewood Cliffs, N.J.: Prentice-Hall, 1971).

[24]Cynthia Fuchs Epstein, *Women's Place: Options and Limits in Professional Careers* (Berkeley: University of California Press, 1970).

[25]See Zillah Eisenstein, ed., *Capitalist Patriarchy and the Case for Socialist Feminism* (New York: Monthly Review Press, 1978).

[26]Cf. Friedrich Engels, *The Origin of the Family, Private Property and the State* (New York: Pathfinder Press, 1972); Marlene Dixon, *Women in Class Struggle*, 2nd ed. (Synthesis Publications, 1980).

[27]Angela Davis, *Women, Race, and Class* (New York: Random House, 1981), p. 228 ff. For an analysis of other ways in which capitalism undermined the black family,

see Jacqueline Jones, *Labor of Love, Labor of Sorrow: Black Women, Work and the Family from Slavery to the Present* (New York: Basic Books, 1985).

[28]See Nancy Hartsock, *Money, Sex, and Power: An Essay on Domination and Community* (New York: Longman, 1981).

[29]Jean Bethke Elshtain, *Public Man, Private Woman: Women in Social and Political Thought* (Princeton, N.J.: Princeton University Press, 1981).

[30]Ibid., p. 322.

[31]See Jean Bethke Elshtain, ed., *The Family in Political Thought* (Amherst, Mass.: University of Massachusetts Press, 1982).

[32]Oates, op. cit., p. 39.

[33]Erik Erikson, *Identity: Youth and Crisis* (New York: Norton, 1968), pp. 25, 246. Cf. Kenneth R. Hoover, *A Politics of Identity: Liberation and the Natural Community* (Urbana, Ill.: University of Illinois Press, 1975), Chaps. 5 and 6. Erikson was widely read by leaders of the black liberation movement, though his ideas on sexual differentiation were controversial among feminists. Cf. Erik Erikson, op. cit., Chap. 8.

NINE

I came to maturity hating the wrongdoers of classic fascism. They were truly hateful. I cannot say that I hate the racists, chauvinists, sexists, polluters, interventionists, price fixers, labor-haters, academic frauds, false patriots and corporate criminals and corrupters who are taking us down the path to friendly fascism. Hatred is *their* game. They hate people at home and abroad, and I suspect many of them hate themselves. . . . They must be fought in the factories and the fields, in the offices and the supermarkets, in the courts and the legislatures, at the ballot boxes, in the classrooms, on the picket lines, in the press and on the airwaves. They must be fought with every nonviolent and nonwarlike means that the ingenuity of man, woman, and child can devise.

Bertram Gross
*Friendly Fascism: The New
Face of Power in America* (1980)

Fascism

The term *fascism* calls up memories of Adolph Hitler and Benito Mussolini and images of totalitarian dictatorship in Germany, Italy, and Japan during the Depression and the Second World War. Interesting as these topics are historically, fascism seems dated as an ideology. Fascism is important not so much because there are active movements by that name, though there are. It is important because through the study of fascism we realize the power of ideas of racism, nationalism, and authoritarianism in whatever form they take—and they take many potent forms in contemporary politics.

Fascism is a combination of racism, nationalism, and authoritarianism that centers on a mystical faith in the superiority of a specific group of people.[1] This definition is illustrated most clearly by German fascism, with its doctrines of Aryan superiority, the historic mission of the Third Reich, and the belief in the *Führer* principle of absolute dictatorship. However, every country influenced by Western civilization has probably had some form of fascist political movement, and the United States is no exception.

Since the perception of wars is mainly shaped by the winners, current generations have come to see fascism as a ridiculous and delusionary ideology. It is hard to see what could have captured the imagination of millions of Germans, Italians, and Japanese and the sympathy, however temporary, of many U.S. editorialists, political leaders, and ordinary citizens. The hardest task of all is to estimate the potential for a fascist revival in current political manifestations of racism, nationalism, and authoritarianism.

We begin, once again, by constructing a vision of a fascist society. Fascists, like Socialists, attempted to form utopian communities.[2] From these experiments, and from the history of fascist thought, we can see what a fascist utopia would be like.

■ A Fascist Utopia

In a famous German propaganda film, *The Triumph of the Will*, there is a scene involving a huge encampment of Nazis at Nuremberg in 1934. Party members are gathered to celebrate the consolidation of power in the hands of Adolph Hitler. Prior to the scenes of massed formations of disciplined followers, there are shots of activities in the camp: early morning exercises, the sharing of work in preparation for the serious ceremonies to follow, roughhouse fun, and hearty meals of sausages and potatoes. In these scenes, the director, Leni Reifenstahl, worked very hard to convey a sense of the happy simplicity, the purity of motive, and the integration of play, work, and loyalty that the Nazis wished to project. The dream of drawing together feelings, beliefs, and everyday activity in one idyllic environment has a powerful fascination. This politics of nostalgia was at the center of the Nazi vision.

What is required to make this vision possible? In the German case, the Nazis thought that a united people, of homogeneous racial background, and having the special character of the common German, the *Volk* ("the people"), was capable of such an existence. The ideology of the *Volk* developed in the revolt against industrialization and democratization that began to affect Germany in the late nineteenth century. The myths of which it was made identified in the German people a native wisdom, a virtuous character, and a feel for the spiritual meaning of life. In Japan, the superiority of the Japanese among Asian peoples was the center of the myth; among Italian fascists, the chauvinism was directed against Africans and, after the alliance with Germany, against Jews.[3]

In the early German fascist utopias, pure Aryans would live together in a kind of rural paradise where land would be provided by the state and all would play their assigned role in its cultivation. Women would bear children, keep the household, and assist their husbands in the work of the community.[4] Men would hold the positions of power. The community would be united in belief in the leader and in common dedication to the protection of the *Volk* from dilution by other races, their customs, and behavior.

The rules of the community would not be the result of bargaining and compromise in a politicized process, but rather of the interpretation of custom and tradition by the leader on behalf of his people. The mythical tradition of racial superiority supplied the symbols and rituals that sanctified the role of the leader as interpreter of the national will. On a more directly political level, the leader works through his most loyal followers, his "bold nucleus" in Mussolini's words, to instill the proper attitudes and virtues in the general population and to help them emulate the model of racial perfection in their daily lives.[5] Membership in the National Socialist Party was, as in the case of the Communist Party, a distinction earned on the basis of loyalty, commitment to the ideal, and willingness to sacrifice everything for the cause.

The focus of politics is on the interpretation of the meaning and mission of the *Volk* rather than on responding to individual desires and settling differences.[6] Character would count for more than reason and logic. Purity of character, the Nazis believed, came from purity of race. The Germans were a special race whose history was seen to have proved that they were capable of great feats of bravery, faith, and the performance of duty. The motto of the Nazi SS was "My loyalty is my honor." There is no room for an independent code of honor or for personal judgment—only loyalty to the *Führer*, leader of the Fatherland.[7]

The *volkisch* community is split neither by racial and ethnic divisions nor by class divisions. Industrialization and democratization were seen paradoxically to have introduced division into society. The emergence of an organized working class, a proletariat, was deeply threatening to the German middle class as well as to the peasants. Such conflict would only divide in the presence of her enemies what was meant to be united: the German people, history's most advanced race. The effort to introduce parliamentary government during the Weimar period accentuated the divisions. The divisive partisan controversies seemed only to discredit the ideal of democracy and confirm the decline of a once unified society.

Yet the Marxist desire for a classless society was even more threatening. Fascists believe that each person has a different level of ability from every other. The point, however, is for each person to give his full effort to whatever part the state requires him or her to play. During the revival of the German Army, privates saluted each other to show that the lower ranks were as worthy of respect as the officers. But to ally with others as a class, and to set that class interest above the interest of the whole community, was perceived as selfish and irresponsible.

The leftist challenge to the unity and organic harmony of German society was particularly unwelcome. The fact that many Communists and Socialists, including Marx, were Jews confirmed the alien character of this development. The fact that class division was most pronounced in cities made the rural orientation of fascist imagery all the more significant.[8]

Fascism manages to combine an appeal to classlessness with extreme authoritarianism. In the fascist utopia there is solidarity but not equality. Solidarity is based on the common commitment to the ideals of the *Volk* rather than on a false leveling.[9] What differentiates people is not so much their individual preferences and styles as their function in the common enterprise. In the Nuremberg rally of 1934, there was a huge formation of workers who performed a military-style rifle drill with their shovels. The ceremony gave to menial labor a special dignity and an identification with the patriotic heroism of the army; the uniforms defined the workers' place in the larger order.

In this context, industrial work was viewed by the Nazis as a new form of craft, and industrial workers were to see themselves as members of a guild of artisans on the medieval model. The notion of a union of workers from different plants advancing their interests at the expense of management was abhorrent to the Nazis.

Genetic Purity, Physical Culture, and the Role of the State

Family life would be structured in the first place by genetic considerations. Only persons of the proper racial stock, excluding Jews, foreigners, and inferior physical specimens, would be encouraged to have children. Indeed, the Nazis set up camps where proper Nordic types could breed more productively than the family structure would allow. Nazi regimes mounted campaigns to reward motherhood with medals, as in a military campaign—the more children, the higher the decoration.

Family relations would be conducted along the lines of fascist belief: the authoritarian position of the father would not be challenged. Mothers would be honored for their carefully circumscribed role as keepers of the home. Children were to be inculcated with the Nazi spirit through home instruction as well as participation in youth clubs, festivals, and ceremonies.

In Nazi Germany, physical culture was considered to be an important part of personal development. Perfection of the body is celebrated above the cultivation of a free intellect. The mind is valued only as it enables the spirit to be understood and translated into practical achievements. Intellectuals who evaluate and criticize are censored, their positions in universities destroyed, and their books burned.

In this closed universe, the spirit of the race is the motivating force, and its indications, as interpreted by the leader and his loyal followers, are the guiding precepts of the community. Any person or practice that does not contribute to this unified effort is beneath contempt and subject to the wrath of the community.

Fascism has its religious characteristics as a system of faith. The faith centers on a myth of the innate superiority of a race and nation. Leaders play the role of priests rather than politicians by presiding at ceremonies, interpreting the myth, and condemning heresies. There are elements of myth in all ideologies, but fascism places the myth at the very core of its ideology.

■ *The Origins of Fascism*

Ernst Cassirer in *The Myth of the State* points out that "myth does not arise solely from intellectual processes; it sprouts forth from deep human emotions."[10] To understand the mythic basis of fascism and of forms of racism and nationalism that lead to authoritarianism, it is important to explore some of the emotions that create the myths.

The common theme of much of the literature that explains why fascism reached such a fever pitch in the 1930s is that it was a response to the devastation of the First World War and the economic crises that followed. Fascist political organizations were founded in Germany, Italy, and Japan in the same year: 1919. In Germany, the loss of face and the destruction of people's savings and investments through inflation in the nineteen twenties and depression of the nineteen thirties created a desperate population bereft of belief and ripe for the assurance that a powerful myth and a skillful leader can provide. For example, in the National Socialist Party's appeal to the voters in the 1932 elections, the connections are direct:

> HITLER is the last hope of those who were deprived of everything: of farm and home, of savings, employment, survival; and who have but one possession left: their faith in a just Germany, which will once again grant to its citizens honor, freedom, and bread.[11]

Scholars who have taken the longer view have pointed to the dislocation caused by the conversion from a traditional peasant society to a modern capitalist economy.[12] As George Mosse points out, the *Volk* movement "used and amplified romanticism to provide an alternative to modernity, to the developing industrial and urban civilization which seemed to rob man of his individual, creative self while cutting him loose from a social order that was seemingly exhausted and lacking vitality."[13] Adolph Hitler presented himself as the personification of both the fall and the rise of the German people.

The elaboration of key elements of the myth preceded Hitler. The proposition that the German people have an historic destiny was rooted in a generation of German philosophy of which the leading figure was Georg Friedrich Hegel (1770–1831). Hegel argued that history is the unfolding of a divine plan by which superior forms of civilization will replace primitive forms. He associated European Christian civilization with this higher level of development.[14] Houston Stewart Chamberlain, the son-in-law of the German composer Richard Wagner, made the link between

Darwinian theory and nationalism at the end of the nineteenth century. Chamberlain argued that a truly superior people proves itself by outdistancing others in production, culture, and military strength. This dubious interpretation of Darwin's scientific conclusions about animal evolution was brought in to bolster the credibility of the myth of Aryan supremacy.[15]

What was seen to have corrupted this special race of people was the influence of foreigners and those lacking in the historical rootedness of the German people. The vast changes that had swept European society in the late nineteenth and early twentieth centuries had undermined the traditional basis of German culture. A rural, aristocratic, religious, and orderly nation was rapidly being overtaken by forces of industrialization, democracy, secularism, and liberality. These changes, felt in every aspect of life, were accentuated by the calamity of the First World War, which had confirmed the downfall of the traditional order. In the economic and social crisis that followed, the search for a scapegoat was on. The Jews, who were seen to represent rootlessness, the commercial spirit, and the urban lifestyle, were accused of undermining the natural state of affairs. They were the enemies, along with the Socialists and Communists, who added the dimensions of secularism and democracy to the disorder of German life.

The revolt against modernity, with its emphasis on mobility, reason, science, and secularism, has preoccupied many analysts of ideology. Research on the personality types most susceptible to the appeal of totalitarianism has indicated a correlation between personal insecurity and a willingness to believe in authoritarian solutions.[16] The pressures on personal life created by rapid change lead to the quest for certainty beyond reason and doubt.

Everyone struggles with the need for belief and commitment. It is belief that sustains people in times of trial and transition. How far into politics the struggle is carried has great impact on the practice of politics.

The combination of modernization and economic collapse that afflicted Italy and Germany after the First World War created a crisis mentality. Socialists offered a critical analysis of Germany's faults. Hitler, on the other hand, provided an impression of certainty and a practical program of reemployment through a military build-up. Although circumstances as extreme as this do not arise in everyone's life, the experience of Nazism makes clear how far such a myth can go in shaping people's political behavior.

There were similar movements in most European countries. The French nationalist ideologist Charles Maurras proposed that the state and the soul are parallel concepts and that the nation is the soul writ large. By this analogy, the state is beyond reason; it is the expression of the enduring meanings of life, and its rituals have a religious quality. Participation in the rituals of the state confers a positive identity on people for whom an identity based on work or personal accomplishment is beyond reach. Nationalism, and through it racism, becomes a recourse against the stresses of modern life.[17]

The *Volk* and the State: National Socialism in Germany

By the construction of a myth about the nation-state, one can respond to feelings of personal helplessness and alienation. Socialists point toward a revolution in the way that production is organized as the key to solving this alienation. Fascists offer a different solution: the submission of individual wills to the will of the state as expressed by its leader—hence the title of the film mentioned earlier, *The Triumph of the Will*. The justification of this "ideology of the will" is that it fulfills the historic mission of Germany, just as the principle of natural selection in Darwinian thought ensures the survival of the fittest. All other aspects of society are to be subordinate to this exercise of, literally, *will* power.[18]

With obedience to the will of the *Führer* as the primary principle, the Nazis in Germany worked toward a theory of commercial organization that would imitate socialism by placing control of key economic decisions in the hands of the state. This is the meaning of *national* socialism, as opposed to democratic socialism. In national socialism, the objective is centralized control of privately owned economic activity on behalf of the national interest. Democratic socialists, by contrast, believe in public ownership of the means of production as a way of increasing people's control over their own lives.

In the effort to establish national socialism, the Nazis received some preliminary support from the organized labor movement. The key issue was: in whose interests was this control to be exercised? It soon became clear that the interests of organized labor were not to be respected, as Hitler moved quickly to destroy the union movement. Those industrialists who did as the Nazis commanded prospered, whereas those who were judged to be unreliable were often deprived of their positions and holdings.[19]

Fascism, Power, and Religion

Fascism characteristically makes a religion out of politics. Regimes in other countries, in the context of the same struggle with modernist tendencies, have tried to make politics into a branch of religion. Communism has its similarities to religion, with its worship of leaders and mythological accounts of the revolution. Iran's fundamentalist religious movement under Ayatollah Khomeini is another example. Public law became the vehicle for the enforcement of the commandments of Islam. It is typical of both strategies that the military comes to be seen as the embodiment of the virtues of the culture—it contains the honor of the nation and the zeal of the religion. Struggle against enemies, and war itself, become the proving grounds of the myth. Military aggression is, for this reason, a common feature of many fascist movements. Japan's fascist regime (1941–1944) was headed by a general, Hideki Tojo. Hitler came to power under the sponsorship of Field Marshal Paul von Hindenburg.

The common characteristic of fascist and religio-political belief systems is, however, that they identify groups of people as the "enemy." Were these beliefs limited to inspiring people to constructive action for the community, they would not be so dangerous. It is one thing to be opposed to tendencies toward impersonalism and modernity, and quite another to visit the blame for these developments on people of another race, creed, or color. Yet most powerful religious and political belief systems seem to do this. For the Nazis, it was the Jews; for the Christian Crusaders in the middle ages, it was the infidels.

The dynamics of scapegoating are an inescapable part of ideologies that rely on the myth of a chosen people. As reality deviates from the myth, the tensions that develop feed the fires of anger toward the "enemy." This dynamic in Germany resulted in the passive acquiescence of millions of people, and the participation of thousands, in the murder of more than six million Jews. Hitler had from the beginning proclaimed his hostility to the Jews, arguing, in a letter to President Hindenburg in 1933, that Jews are "an entirely alien body, which has never really become one with the German people."[20] Whatever went wrong in Germany, including the defeat in the First World War, could be blamed on the Jews.

The core of fascism was the *Führer* principle: the *Führer* is the purest manifestation of the will of the race.[21] It was with this principle that both Germany and Italy were led into an unreal world where morality gave way to sadistic manipulation and barbaric destruction. The themes their leaders used—nationalism and racism—do not lend themselves very well to solving the issues of politics and the economy. In the end, German, Italian, and Japanese fascism as ideologies were little more than justifications of the power of the leader and his party. Fascist doctrines concerning the economy, the role of the state, the position of labor, and the responsibilities of business all gave way to the expediencies of preserving power.[22] Beyond an initial mobilization, the everyday realities of people's lives could not be improved by extolling the virtues of a nation or the superiority of a race.

Fascism in the United States

Although there is a long history of racist, nationalist, and authoritarian politics in the United States, little success has been achieved by any movement identified as fascist. The reason is the difficulty of combining all three elements within the American context. Just as Socialists have difficulty organizing class-based politics in a dispersed and diverse population, so Fascists have a problem with securing allegiance to one ethnic and racial group among many.

The effort to create a German Bund in the United States modeled on Hitler's National Socialist Party was a dismal failure.[23] Elements of the Ku Klux Klan who organized themselves into the Black Legion, a militant white supremacist corps, were long on mysticism and short on effective political action.[24] The American Nazi Party under the leadership of George Lincoln Rockwell has never attracted more than a few hundred followers. More significant are religious fundamentalists who advocate authoritarian solutions to America's various crises and proclaim the innate superiority of Christian, or lately Islamic, peoples. Not all of these appeals lead to fascism; it is the mix of religion and authoritarian political solutions that contains the potential for fascist politics.

In the words of two scholars who surveyed the entire history of right-wing extremism in the United States, "the American population is still highly vulnerable to political extremism; the American political system is less vulnerable, but scarcely fail-safe."[25] The reason for this vulnerability is the high level of insecurity in American life. The anxiety and dislocation caused by a fast-paced competitive economy create the environment for scapegoating. Conspiracy theories directed at races, ethnic groups, and cliques, at women and unpopular leaders, provide easy recourse when times are hard and personal circumstances are difficult. The more unstable the environment is perceived to be, the greater the danger of extremism and the more likely that unprincipled demagogues will profit from people's need to believe.

The signs of this phenomenon in U.S. political life are many. The periodic waves of "Red Scares," in which all those who disagree with the prevailing social wisdom are branded as communist sympathizers; demagoguery based on racism; and theories of conspiracy on the part of Jews or foreign elements all have a rich history. The mythological character of these episodes is demonstrated by the lack of connection to verifiable evidence. There may have been a small number of believers in communism in positions of influence in the United States in the 1950s, but Senator Joseph McCarthy never found one of them as a result of his famous investigations. Yet his power over public opinion was enormous, and it was used to destroy the reputations and careers of hundreds of innocent people who were merely accused, without proof, of "anti-Americanism."[26]

Theories of ethnicism, racism, or historical conspiracy do not withstand rational analysis. The interpersonal variation in mental and physical ability among people of a given race always outweighs the average differences *between* races. Conspiracy theories fail to be credible when large decisions are involved because of the number of people that would have to maintain secrecy. Yet the temptation to resolve the difficulties of modern life by these simple means remains.

In contemporary society, with the complexity of relations among huge centers of economic, political, and cultural power, it is less likely that fascism would resemble its classic form. The channels of communication are far more diverse, the sources of criticism more numerous, and democratic traditions stronger than they were in Western Europe and the Orient in the twenties and thirties. Yet Bertram Gross, in his *Friendly Fascism: The New Face of Power in America*, argues that there is a new variety of fascism that is on the rise.[27] "Friendly" fascism achieves some of the same results as the classic variety, but the means are different.

Rather than employing force, friendly fascism uses the media to divert attention through displays of sex and violence, manipulate feelings through symbolic appeals to patriotism and religion, and shape opinion so as to isolate dissenters. The technology of surveillance and the authorization of increasing leeway for security agencies provide more direct means of disabling the opposition. The organizational vehicle of friendly fascism is the corporation rather than the political party. The aim is the hegemony of large corporations rather than the *Volk* or the military, though appeals to both are part of its approach.[28]

Gross does not claim that the United States has arrived at friendly fascism yet, or that its advance is the work of a simple conspiracy. The resistance to authoritarianism is deeply ingrained in this culture. Yet he sees the *logic* of technology, and the class interest of corporate managers, taking us in this direction. His fundamental concern is the weakening of democratic attitudes and what he perceives as the decline in effective participation in major decisions by the American people. Gross's scenario for fascism is harder to evaluate than the classic pattern, since the forces at work are by their very nature less visible. The verification of this theory depends on a careful and realistic assessment of the status of people's security and liberties.

Another perspective on the current danger arising from fascism comes from the work of A. James Gregor. In his *The Fascist Persuasion in Radical Politics*, Gregor points out that many movements identifying themselves as Marxist are better conceived of as fascist. He suggests that "Karl Marx would have found very little in the political culture and political institutions of Cuba, China, or Russia that he could identify as Marxist."[29] The symbolism of Marx's class-based revolution has been borrowed to justify the sort of authoritarian statism that fascists advocate directly.

■ Conclusion

The decline of meaningful public involvement in decision making is the universal characteristic of fascism. The Nazis created the illusion of participation through parades and plebiscites. The purpose of this show was the opposite of real participation. As A. F. K. Organski points out,

> Political mobilization serves the double function of disciplining the masses into an attitude of obedience in which non-participation in decision-making is taken for granted and becomes a virtue, and of further disciplining them into an attitude receptive to making sacrifices. At the same time, the attention of the mobilized population is directed away from their grievances and channeled into harmless political activity.[30]

In reality, "classic fascism" meant rule by a tiny group of ruthless demagogues. Nevertheless, the illusion of participation is the subtlest aspect of fascism. By appealing to the need to belong, to be included, to feel the strength of solidarity, fascism taps a powerful current in people's lives. If, at the same time, it promises deliverance from economic crises and relief from the pressures of modernity, the loss of effective participation is not so obvious.[31] It is the difference between the appearance and the reality of participation in power that is the measure of fascism, whether classic or contemporary.

■ *Notes*

[1]This descriptive definition follows from the work of George Mosse, *The Crisis of German Ideology: Intellectual Origins of the Third Reich* (New York: Grosset and Dunlap, 1964) and A. James Gregor, *The Ideology of Fascism* (New York: Free Press, 1969), pp. 10–15. For a review of the controversy over the definition of fascism, see Gilbert Allardyce, "What Fascism Is Not: Thoughts on the Definition of a Concept," and the responses by Stanley Payne and Ernst Nolte, in the *American Historical Review* 84 (1979):367–398.

[2]See Mosse, op. cit., Chap. 6.

[3]See Bertram Gross's summary of the comparative development of the three "classic fascisms" in *Friendly Fascism: The New Face of Power in America* (Boston: South End Press, 1980), pp. 11–31.

[4]On the role of women in Nazi Germany, see Jill Stephenson, *The Nazi Organization of Women* (Totowa, N.J.: Barnes and Noble, 1981).

[5]Ernst Nolte, *Three Faces of Fascism* (New York: Holt, Rinehart & Winston, 1966), p. 158.

[6]See Hannah Arendt's discussion of law in a totalitarian society, in *The Origins of Totalitarianism* (Cleveland: World Press, 1958), p. 462.

[7]On the role of the cult of the strong leader in rendering political participation meaningless, see Piero Melograni, "The Cult of the Duce in Mussolini's Italy," in George Mosse, ed., *International Fascism: New Thoughts and New Approaches* (Beverly Hills, Calif.: Sage Publications, 1979).

[8]Mosse, *The Crisis of German Ideology*, p. 22.

[9]Arendt, op. cit., pp. 360–361.

[10]Ernst Cassirer, *The Myth of the State* (New Haven: Yale University Press, 1946), pp. 46–47.

[11]Joachim Remak, *The Nazi Years: A Documentary History* (New York: Prentice-Hall, 1969), p. 42.

[12]For a statement of the "modernization" thesis concerning the rise of fascism, see Peter Stearns, *European Society in Upheaval* (New York: Macmillan, 1975), p. 2. Cf. David Schoenbaum, *Hitler's Social Revolution: Class and Status in Nazi Germany, 1933–1939* (New York: Doubleday, 1980), pp. 13–15.

[13]Mosse, *The Crisis of German Ideology*, p. 17.

[14]Marx was also a student of Hegel, but Marx thought that history revealed itself not through the spirit as expressed in culture and the actions of leaders but through the process of production. It was revolutions in the relationship between the productive process and the class system that would bring about a higher level of development, not the leadership of a *Führer*.

[15]In the ideology of the *Volk*, the Aryans were portrayed as a people originating in India who had found their way westward to Europe, developing in the process traits of strength and self-reliance, and who served as the racial stock for the Nordic races and the Anglo-Saxons. Mosse, *The Crisis of German Ideology*, pp. 88–90.

[16]T. W. Adorno et. al., *The Authoritarian Personality* (New York: Harper, 1950), pp. 753–783.

[17]Nolte, op. cit., p. 103. Hitler maintained that "The state is only the means to an end. The end is: Conservatism of race." Cited in Arendt, op. cit., p. 357.

[18]J. P. Stern, *Hitler: The Führer and the People* (Los Angeles: University of California Press, 1975), pp. 68–77.

[19]David Schoenbaum, *Hitler's Social Revolution: Class and Status in Nazi Germany* (New York: Doubleday Anchor, 1967), pp. 77–158. Schoenbaum points out that "With the demolition of the unions and the introduction of the law on 'The Organization of National Labor,' business exchanged the pressure of the unions

for the pressure of the State." Control over managerial decisions was lost to the Nazis. Ibid., p. 157.

[20]Remak, op. cit., p. 147.

[21]Stern, op. cit., pp. 130–134.

[22]Arendt, op. cit., p. 404. Cf. Schoenbaum, op. cit., pp. 155–158, and Ivone Kirkpatrick, *Mussolini: A Study in Power* (New York: Avon, 1964), p. 175.

[23]Sander Diamond, *The Nazi Movement in the United States, 1924–1941* (Ithaca, N.Y.: Cornell University Press, 1974).

[24]Peter Amann, "Vigilante Fascism: The Black Legion," *Comparative Studies in Society and History* 25, no. 3 (1983):490–524.

[25]Seymour Martin Lipset and Earl Raab, *The Politics of Unreason: Right Wing Extremism in America, 1790–1970* (New York: Harper & Row, 1970), p. 508.

[26]See Thomas Reeves, *The Life and Times of Joe McCarthy: A Biography* (New York: Stein & Day, 1983); Walter Goodman, *The Committee: The Extraordinary Career of the House Committee on Un-American Activities* (New York: Farrar, Straus & Giroux, 1968).

[27]Gross, op. cit. Cf. Zbigniew Brzezinski, *Between Two Ages: America's Role in the Technetronic Era* (New York: Vintage, 1970).

[28]See Gross's comparison of "friendly" with "classic" fascism, op. cit., p. 171, and his account of how we have not yet arrived at friendly fascism on pp. 344–345.

[29]A. James Gregor, *The Fascist Persuasion in Radical Politics* (Princeton, N.J.: Princeton University Press, 1974), p. 395.

[30]A. F. K. Organski, "Fascism and Modernization," in S. J. Woolf, ed., *The Nature of Fascism* (New York: Random House, 1968), p. 33.

[31]Cf. George Mosse, "Introduction: A General Theory of Fascism," in Mosse, *International Fascism*, pp. 1–41.

TEN

Assessing the population, checking up on it, is a principal and never-ending social activity in Communist countries. If a painter is to have an exhibition, an ordinary citizen to receive a visa to a country with a sea coast, a soccer player to join the national team, then a vast array of recommendations and reports must be garnered (from the concierge, colleagues, the police, the local Party organization, the pertinent trade union) and added up, weighed, and summarized by special officials. These reports have nothing to do with artistic talent, kicking ability, or maladies that respond well to salt sea air; they deal with one thing only: the "citizen's political profile" (in other words, what the citizen says, what he thinks, how he behaves, how he acquits himself at meetings or May Day parades).

Milan Kundera
The Unbearable Lightness of Being (1984)

The Future of Ideology

Other countries might see their governments harassing dissidents and trying to drive them out of existence, but America—it was said—tolerated diversity as much as possible. Since ideas like these were simply untrue, once the blinders were lifted, the structure fell. Suddenly, numbers of people discovered that, in many ways, the history of the United States is a history of repression. The U.S. government has hassled workers, Indians, blacks, women, left-wingers, right-wingers, immigrants. In this century alone there have been two Red scares, concentration camps, guilt by association, deportations, preventive detention, political espionage—all carried on by a government supposedly dedicated to freedom.

Alan Wolfe
The Seamy Side of Democracy (1973)

Power is an inescapable part of people's lives. There are few aspects of our relations with others that are more vexing. When the problem of power is moved from the interpersonal level to the realm of communities and states, most people see its realities only indirectly. Perceptions are too often shaped by the media and by what leaders would like us to think.

As for people's beliefs about politics, they are sometimes more a reflection of personal needs for reassurance, or outlets for aggression, than a judgment based on careful thought and analysis. A casual understanding of ideology can amplify the risk of misjudgment. Yet, for all these limitations, people solve problems of power and freedom every day in ways that generate creativity and improvement for themselves and others, whether personally or at the level of a community and even a nation.

There is great wisdom about the uses of power in the ideologies we have examined, but the wisdom has to be rescued from simplifications and dangerous illusions. Ideologies begin from models of life that can too easily become stereotypes. In classical liberalism, the ideal of the autonomous, freely choosing individual carries with it none of the complexity of human interdependence with society and the environment. Taken at face value, it is an invitation to license and the disintegration of community. C. B. Macpherson argues that the concept of "possessive individualism" at the heart of classical liberalism, and now of libertarian conservatism, takes us straight into a dilemma from which there is no escape:

> As soon as you make the essential human quality the striving for possessions rather than creative activity, you are caught up in an insoluble contradiction. Human beings are sufficiently unequal in strength and skill that if you put them into an unlimited contest for possessions, some will not only get more than others, but will get control of the means of labour to which the others must have access. The others then cannot be fully human even in the restricted sense of being able to get possessions, let alone in the original sense of being able to use their faculties in purposive creative activity. So in choosing to make the essence of man the striving for possessions, we make it impossible for many men to be fully human.[1]

If the starting point is a simple belief in individual freedom, and if this is followed through to the organization of a purely utilitarian state based on private property, then the path leads directly to the domination of some individuals by others—and to the destruction of the original ideal of freedom for all.

Similarly, communitarian ideologies depend upon conceptions of community that can be reduced to caricatures of harmony and cooperation. What Eugene Kamenka suggests about socialist conceptions of the general will could be said of any communitarian ideology, whether it be socialist, communist, traditional conservative, or fascist:

> Precisely because socialists can still give no coherent content to that central concept of the general will as a truly universal will or to the social interest as something in which all individual interests can be reconciled and brought to agreement, the concept of community remains in socialism important but fundamentally incoherent. It operates usefully as a critical idea, like alienation, against which particular realities can be judged. But when it is treated as something that can be brought into reality in a specific sense, sharply defined, it becomes brutal, oppressive and intolerable.[2]

Just as simple individualism can disguise a process of domination, so an illusory "general will" can be made into a mask for tyranny.

The answers to these ideological simplifications and illusions lie in the future as well as in the past. If classical liberalism is carefully examined, there is more to be found than simple individualism. As we saw in Chapter Two, there is Jefferson's notion that individuality carries with it the Creator's intention that the real purpose of each person's unique talents should be to complement the talents of others in building a society. In that respect, the community has rights too—the right to expect the best effort of all concerned—and the duty to provide what is necessary for that to happen. There are similar insights in Locke, Mill, and Green and in contemporary thinkers about the classical and reform liberal traditions.

As for the communitarian image of the "general will," Rousseau never argued that the general will could be imposed on any society. Rather, he suggested that individuals might be brought into harmony with others in circumstances where they felt free, secure, involved in making crucial decisions, and on reasonably equal footing with others in a material sense. These conditions, not the precise definition of an abstract general will, are the keys that open the door to community. In the history of communitarian thought there are manifold speculations and reports of experimentation with these and other proposed conditions. Some of them are reviewed in each chapter. To go beyond an introductory text and read these insights in the original is to participate in a great and fateful conversation that has been going on for centuries.

The history of political philosophy suggests that, in times of political crisis, powerful new systems of ideas can be created by theorists sensitive to developments around them and original enough to synthesize ideas into terms that communicate new understandings for cultures in need of answers. Classical liberalism received its most powerful formulation in the century of England's great Civil War, the seventeenth century. Both the Declaration of Independence and the *Communist Manifesto* were written in the midst of revolutionary fervor. Even greater works were written as sweeping changes of a cultural and economic character came to the surface of society and were captured in the writings of great political theorists.

The future of ideology is not in the rehashing of old stereotypes packaged with appealing symbols for mass consumption. The future is in the escape from these simple images toward a more mature and intelligent understanding of life, of power, and of the potential of politics for the improvement of society. While they are still in their formative stages, some of the liberation ideologies discussed in Chapter Eight have tried to build bridges between individualist and communitarian ideologies through a new understanding of the social and political requirements for humane personal development.

Yet the creation of a society cannot be merely the work of its politicians, or its scholars. All the hopeful ideals of political philosophy, whether individualist or communitarian, rest on the thoughtful engagement of the individual. Those who command the greatest power in a society, whether through force or intellect, are usually nothing more than adept followers of the public will. The will of the people must be formed out of the common sense and careful thought of the citizens, or no amount of clever rationalizing, and no quantity of arms, will save society in the end. The alternative to humane understanding is authoritarianism and the abdication of individual participation to manipulation and domination by others.

Politics is important not just because governments command armies and collect taxes. As we have seen in the study of ideologies, beliefs about politics are linked to the human quest for meaning in life. Ideology is tied to the personal need for identity, and the development of identity is as fundamental a process of life as physical survival. The search for meaning will be served by propaganda, stereotypes, and symbolic manipulation if it is not served by our best judgment. As Hannah Arendt observed in *The Origins of Totalitarianism:*

> Before mass leaders seize the power to fit reality to their lies, their propaganda is marked by its extreme contempt for facts as such, for in their opinion fact depends entirely on the power of [the] man who can fabricate it.[3]

The human quest for meaning will be served in one way or another. An ideology is not a luxury or the ornament of a well-educated mind. Whether consciously or not, ideology forms a part of every person's life. The only question is whether it is well considered, open to verification through the best application of knowledge, faith, and judgment, and appropriate to the times and to one's experience of society.

■ *Notes*

[1]C. B. Macpherson, *The Real World of Democracy* (New York: Oxford University Press, 1965), p. 54.

[2]Eugene Kamenka, *Community as a Social Ideal* (New York: St. Martin's Press, 1982), p. 26.

[3]Hannah Arendt, *The Origins of Totalitarianism*, 2nd ed. (Cleveland: World Publishing Company, 1958), p. 350.

BIBLIOGRAPHY

The footnotes for each chapter contain suggestions on readings that follow up on specific arguments. The purpose of this bibliography is to suggest a few sources, some of them previously mentioned in other connections, that will broaden the reader's general understanding of political ideologies.

Hannah Arendt. *The Origins of Totalitarianism.* Cleveland: World Press, 1958.

Bernard Bailyn. *The Ideological Origins of the American Revolution.* Cambridge, Mass.: Belknap Press, 1967.

Terence Ball. *Political Theory and Praxis: New Perspectives.* Minneapolis, Minn.: University of Minnesota Press, 1977.

Jane Bayes. *Minority Politics and Ideologies in the United States.* San Francisco: Chandler and Sharp, 1982.

Carl Becker. *The Heavenly City of the Eighteenth Century Philosophers.* New Haven: Yale University Press, 1932.

Samuel Beer. *Britain against Itself: The Political Contradictions of Collectivism.* New York: Norton, 1982.

Murray Bookchin. *The Ecology of Freedom: The Emergence and Dissolution of Hierarchy.* Palo Alto, Calif.: Cheshire Books, 1982.

Daniel Boorstin. *The Lost World of Thomas Jefferson.* Boston: Beacon Press, 1948.

David Caute. *The Left in Europe: Since 1789.* New York: McGraw-Hill, 1966.

William Connolly. *The Terms of Political Discourse,* 2nd ed. Princeton, N.J.: Princeton University Press, 1983.

John Diggins. *The American Left in the Twentieth Century.* New York: Harcourt Brace Jovanovich, 1973.

Louis Dumont. *From Mandeville to Marx: The Genesis and Triumph of Economic Ideology.* Chicago: University of Chicago Press, 1977.

Murray Edelman. *Politics As Symbolic Action: Mass Arousal and Quiescence.* Madison, Wis.: Institute for Research on Poverty Monograph, 1971.

Jean Bethke Elshtain, ed. *The Family in Political Thought.* Amherst, Mass.: University of Massachusetts Press, 1982.

Sara Evans. *Personal Politics: The Roots of Women's Liberation in the Civil Rights Movement and the New Left.* New York: Knopf, 1979.

Robert Booth Fowler. *Believing Skeptics: American Political Intellectuals.* New York: Greenwood Press, 1978.

Lawrence Goodwyn. *Democratic Promise: The Populist Movement in America*. New York: Oxford University Press, 1976.

Philip Green. *The Pursuit of Inequality*. New York: Random House, 1981.

Louis Hartz. *The Liberal Tradition in America: An Interpretation of American Political Thought since the Revolution*. New York: Harcourt, 1955.

Christopher Hill. *The World Turned Upside Down: Radical Ideas during the English Revolution*. London: Penguin, 1972.

Albert Hirschman. *The Passions and the Interests: Political Arguments for Capitalism before Its Triumph*. Princeton, N.J.: Princeton University Press, 1977.

Lewis Hyde. *The Gift: Imagination and the Erotic Life of Property*. New York: Random House, 1979.

Eugene Kamenka. *Community as a Social Ideal*. New York: St. Martin's Press, 1983.

Mark Kann. *The American Left: Failures and Fortunes*. New York: Praeger, 1982.

Russell Kirk. *The Conservative Mind: From Burke to Eliot*, 3rd ed. Chicago: Regnery, 1960.

Sidney Lens. *Radicalism in America*. New York: Crowell, 1969.

Seymour Martin Lipset and Earl Raab. *The Politics of Unreason: Right Wing Extremism in America, 1790–1970*. New York: Harper & Row, 1970.

Staughton Lynd. *The Intellectual Origins of American Radicalism*. Cambridge, Mass.: Harvard University Press, 1982.

Tibor Machan and M. Bruce Johnson. *Rights and Regulation: Ethical, Political, and Economic Issues*. New York: Ballinger, 1983.

Douglas MacLean and Claudia Mills, eds. *Liberalism Reconsidered*. Totowa, N.J.: Rowman and Allenhead, 1983.

C. B. Macpherson. *The Real World of Democracy*. New York: Oxford University Press, 1965.

Kingsley Martin. *The Rise of French Liberal Thought: A Study of Political Ideas from Bayle to Condorcet*, 2nd ed., 1954. J. P. Mayer, ed., Greenwood Press, 1980.

Bruce Mazlish. *James and John Stuart Mill*. New York: Basic Books, 1962.

David McLellan. *The Thought of Karl Marx*. New York: Harper & Row, 1971.

Linda Medcalf and Kenneth Dolbeare. *Neopolitics: American Political Ideas in the 1980's*. New York: Random House, 1985.

David Milton. *The Politics of U.S. Labor: From the Great Depression to the New Deal*. New York: Monthly Review Press, 1982.

George Nash. *The Conservative Intellectual Movement in America since 1945*. New York: Basic Books, 1979.

Robert Nisbet. *The Quest for Community*. New York: Oxford University Press, 1962.

Michael Novak. *The Spirit of Democratic Capitalism*. New York: Simon & Schuster, 1982.

Stephen Oates. *Let the Trumpet Sound: The Life of Martin Luther King*. New York: Mentor, 1982.

Michael Oakeshott. *Rationalism in Politics*. London: Methuen, 1962.

Bertell Ollman. *Alienation: Marx's Conception of Man in Capitalist Society*, 2nd ed. Cambridge: Cambridge University Press, 1976.

Terry Perlin, ed. *Contemporary Anarchism*. San Francisco, Calif.: Transaction Books, 1979.

Ralph Pettman. *Biopolitics and International Values: Investigating Liberal Norms*. Elmsford, N.Y.: Pergamon Press, 1981.

Raymond Plant. "Community: Concept, Conception, and Ideology," *Politics and Society*, vol. 8, no. 1 (1978):79–107.

Karl Polanyi. *Great Transformation: The Political and Economic Origins of Our Time*. Boston: Beacon Press, 1957 (1944).

John Rawls. *A Theory of Justice.* Cambridge, Mass.: Harvard University Press, 1971.

Stanley Rothman and Robert Licther. *Roots of Radicalism: Jews, Christians, and the New Left.* New York: Oxford, 1982.

Michael Sandel. *Liberalism and the Limits of Justice.* Cambridge: Cambridge University Press, 1982.

John Schwarz. *America's Hidden Success: A Reassessment of Twenty Years of Public Policy.* New York: Norton, 1983.

Thomas Landon Thorson. *The Logic of Democracy.* New York: Holt, 1962.

Garry Wills. *Confessions of a Conservative.* New York: Penguin, 1979.

Sheldon Wolin. *Politics and Vision: Continuity and Innovation in Western Political Thought.* Boston: Little, Brown, 1960.

Howard Zinn. *A People's History of the United States.* New York: Harper & Row, 1980.

Robert Zwier. *Born-Again Politics: The New Christian Right in America.* InterVarsity Press, 1982.

Reading the classics of political theory in the original (or in an English translation where appropriate) is usually the best way to explore these ideas. Your library will have various editions, generally with helpful introductions, of the works of the theorists cited in this book. For assistance in understanding particular theorists, consult the following sources.

Martin Carnoy. *The State and Political Theory.* Princeton, N.J.: Princeton University Press, 1984.

Kenneth Dolbeare. *American Political Thought.* Chatham, N.J.: Chatham House, 1984.

Frank and Fritzie Manuel. *Utopian Thought in the Western World.* Cambridge, Mass.: Belknap Press, 1982.

George H. Sabine and Thomas Landon Thorson. *A History of Political Theory,* 4th ed. Hinsdale, Ill.: Dryden Press, 1973.

Mulford Q. Sibley. *Political Ideas and Ideologies: A History of Political Thought.* New York: Harper & Row, 1970.

James Wiser. *Political Philosophy: A History of the Search for Order.* Englewood Cliffs, N.J.: Prentice-Hall, 1983.

INDEX